T0083106

"I was fortunate to work with Bob Neuschel extensively early in my career. He inculcated the philosophy and values of 'Servant Leadership' to his newest associates from day one. That legacy has been an important foundation for my own leadership approach. I commend the lessons of his book with the highest respect and enthusiasm."

—LEO F. MULLIN
Former Chairman and Chief Executive Officer, Delta Air Lines, Inc.

"Bob Neuschel is a great student of leadership and his book needs to be read by all those seriously interested in this important subject."

—P. S. WILLMOTT
Former President and Chief Executive Officer, Zenith Electronics Corporation

"As the pace of business has accelerated with new technologies and worldwide markets, Professor Neuschel's concept of the Servant Leader is more relevant than ever. We must have more capable, empowered people throughout our business enterprises, and those can only be developed by truly embracing and practicing Servant Leadership."

—DAVID R. HOLMES
Former Chairman, The Reynolds and Reynolds Company

"Bob Neuschel has a very clear concept about the role of the leader in our free enterprise system. Leadership is a key productivity factor and thus raises the standard of living but, simultaneously, he recognizes the key quality of leadership: the love and care for others is the critical element. The results are human productivity, but equally important, personal growth of the participant."

—DON SCHNEIDER
Chairman of the Board of Directors, Schneider National, Inc.

"Bob Neuschel has exemplified the principles of leadership in his personal and professional life. His coverage of leadership is a primer for success in life as well as in business. Now he helps us to understand how we too may be effective 'Servant Leaders.'"

—C. JOHN LANGLEY, JR.
Distinguished Professor of Logistics and Transportation, College of Business Administration, University of Tennessee

"I have worked with Professor Bob Neuschel for twenty-five years and watched as students and alumni continue to flock to his classes and office seeking his wisdom on leadership. Now Bob shares much of that knowledge in this insightful new book, *The Servant Leader: Unleashing the Power of Your People.* This book is a must-read for leaders and teachers of leadership worldwide."

—DONALD P. JACOBS
Dean Emeritus, Kellogg Graduate School of Management,
Northwestern University

"Bob Neuschel has devoted his life to the study of leadership and is one of the great authorities on the subject. His insights into the leadership challenges of the twenty-first century provide crystal-clear evidence that the true measure of any leader is the ability to facilitate the development of others."

—DAVID R. GOODE
Chairman and Chief Executive Officer, Norfolk Southern Corporation

"Professor Neuschel's sessions on leadership are always highly rated by managers in our Executive Development Program. And my university students regard his visits as a special event. Now Bob's wisdom is readily available to all those who are interested in knowing more about this critical topic."

—DOUGLAS M. LAMBERT
Raymond E. Mason Chair in Transportation and Logistics,
Ohio State University

THE SERVANT LEADER

THE SERVANT LEADER

Unleashing the Power of Your People

ROBERT P. NEUSCHEL

NORTHWESTERN
UNIVERSITY PRESS

**KOGAN
PAGE**

✝

IN MEMORIAM

ROBERT PERCY NEUSCHEL

1919–2004

Soldier, consultant, teacher, father,
husband, and servant leader extraordinaire

Publisher's note

Every possible effort has been made to ensure that the information contained in this book is accurate at the time of going to press, and the publishers and authors cannot accept responsibility for any errors or omissions, however caused. No responsibility for loss or damage occasioned to any person acting, or refraining from action, as a result of the material in this publication can be accepted by the editor, the publisher, or any of the authors.

Northwestern University Press
Evanston, Illinois 60208-4170
ISBN 0-8101-2339-8

Kogan Page Limited
London N1 9JN, United Kingdom
ISBN 0 7494 4533 5

Printed in the United States of America

10   9   8   7   6   5   4   3   2   1

Copyright © 2005 by Virginia Maxwell Neuschel. First published 1998 by Visions Sports Management Group, Inc. Northwestern University Press edition published 2005. All rights reserved.

Library of Congress Cataloging-in-Publication Data

Neuschel, Robert P. (Robert Percy), 1919-
  The servant leader : unleashing the power of your people / Robert P. Neuschel.
    p. cm.
  ISBN 0-8101-2339-8 (pbk. : alk. paper)
  1. Leadership. I. Title.
HD57.7.N48 2005
658.4'092--dc22
                              2005016289

British Library Cataloging Data

A CIP record for this book is available from the British Library.

∞ The paper used in this publication meets the minimum requirements of the American National Standard for Information Sciences —Permanence of Paper for Printed Library Materials, ANSI Z39.48-1992.

This book is dedicated with grateful thanks and love to Virginia Neuschel, my wife of many years. For over half a century she has been my great supporter and a helpful, honest but gentle, critic. She has been a true inspiration for me and this book because she herself embodies so many of the fine qualities of the servant leader.

CONTENTS

Bob Neuschel learned lifelong lessons about leadership the hard way more than a half a century ago.

"One of the finest servant leaders I have ever known was an infantry captain I served under who was training us back in the summer of 1941 for the war which broke out a few months later," he writes.

"He was incredibly tough on us, and demanded the utmost in discipline and performance, and many of us, unused to military life, characterized him as rough and tough, unreasonably harsh, and almost cruel. At first most of us hated his guts."

But it wasn't long before Bob and his buddies had a change of heart.

"We learned that he had only two objectives and they were simple but not necessarily easy to achieve—to make you guys the best fighters in the world and increase your chances of coming back alive and well."

"The captain could have gotten by with demanding less from us and it would have meant less work for him. But he had a compelling desire to help us become the best, to come out a winner and stay alive —the true mark of a servant leader."

More than fifty years after he was "broken in" by that tough captain, Bob Neuschel has issued America a wake-up call as clear and compelling as the blast of a trumpet at reveille: it is time to revitalize the concept of leadership in our society and confront a serious shortage of quality leaders in all of our institutions.

Yet while forcefully pounding home this theme, the author shows little patience for hand-wringing. Diagnosis delivered, Bob moves quickly to the cure.

Drawing upon decades of experience in the military, as an international management consultant, and as a professor at one of our finest universities, he skillfully delineates the most vital qualities of leadership. And by citing examples from a vast array of fields—business, politics, sports, religion, even war—he makes those qualities come alive. Reading this book, I now know why Bob Neuschel is so effective and admired as a teacher. He does not preach or lecture; he instead portrays the qualities of leadership in the most appealing terms, so that we can't help but want to search for and develop those qualities in ourselves. He is a very skillful motivational coach!

For those of us responsible for leading institutions, *The Servant Leader* tackles some tough questions. For example, is it possible to be a great leader and a bad manager—or vice versa? Which is more important? Bob's discussions of the concept of "managerial leadership"—a unified set of skills that both provides an organization with a vision, along with the necessary managerial attention to make that vision achievable—shows us a path out of this quandary.

Manager/leaders must develop and articulate a sense of mission, the author explains, but must also listen and be accessible and know how to sweep the clutter of unimportant activities aside in order to focus on the big questions.

Success at managerial leadership requires not only an ability to motivate others, but a high level of self-management as well. An effective leader must have achieved a significant level of personal maturity, be reasonably well-adjusted to life, and be able to manage one's emotions. This is wise counsel. It's hard to manage others if you can't manage yourself.

Perhaps most significantly—for it speaks directly to the central concern of this book—Bob Neuschel believes that the most important responsibility of a leader is "renewal." You are not really a leader unless you are developing other leaders within your organization to provide room for both growth and continuity when you are gone.

That's advice we've all heard before. But what distinguishes Bob's discussion is that he presents this responsibility not as a managerial burden, but as a wonderful opportunity and a noble calling. The leadership class of our country need not be an elite group, he exhorts us.

There are so many more people with the potential to be good leaders than we realize. We must seek them out and develop them.

Such is the noble calling of the "servant leader"—one who "has followers whom he helps to grow in stature, capacity, or in some way contributes to building them into more useful and satisfied people." Speaking for myself, nothing I have ever done has been more rewarding to me personally than the opportunities I have had to mentor young people and watch them grow into leaders.

In the final analysis, even as clear-thinking and astute an expert as Bob acknowledges that the foundation of leadership is "more judgment than knowledge, more art than science." In the opening pages of *The Servant Leader,* the author quotes James MacGregor Burns, who once called leadership "a baffling subject." By the end of the book, you'll find this vital subject considerably less baffling—a profound contribution as our nation and its institutions stare out at the uncharted terrain of a new millennium.

Thomas J. Donohue
President and CEO
U.S. Chamber of Commerce
1998

My first impressive lesson in *servant leadership* took place early in my military career at the beginning of World War II. I shall never forget Commanding General Lear of the Second Army speaking to several hundred newly commissioned second lieutenants, of which I was one. His words are still fresh in my mind even after the fifty-seven years since our graduation ceremony. The general quickly and simply stated his leadership philosophy: "Always *serve* your troops first that you may command them better." He went on to challenge us to always "Feed your troops and they will fight like hell for you. And when I say feed, I don't mean just the belly, but that is important. I also mean to feed the mind, the heart, and the spirit. In fact, *grow the total soldier.*" I have adopted and tailored his philosophy to my subsequent management consulting, corporate boards, and university careers. I have often counseled corporate executives to always *grow the total person.* It is universally true that as you help people grow you not only enable them to produce more but in the process increase their personal satisfaction and well-being because they have the joy of making a greater contribution. Therein lies the motivation to *unleash the power of your people* and your organization.

Because of my deep convictions of the great power for good that results from the servant leader concept I felt compelled to put my story into *this* book—*The Servant Leader: Unleashing the Power of Your People.* My fervent desire is that in a small way it will motivate our leaders to *first serve* that *they may lead better.* In this way the book will hopefully help our leaders *unleash the power of their people* as they mature into *servant leaders.* That is the simple and compelling motivation for this book.

Robert P. Neuschel
January 8, 1998

ACKNOWLEDGMENTS

The list of distinguished people to whom I am indebted is very, very long. In the limited space allotted me at the front of this book, let me mention just a few from that long list.

Many military leaders helped to shape my early thinking about the art and science of leadership. To represent them all, let me thank Lt. General Ben Lear for the leadership wisdom he and many other senior officers imparted to this young Army soldier and officer. Following World War II and down through the years, I had the great privilege and good fortune to work with and learn from some splendid servant leaders. At the head of that list were Leo F. Mullin, President and CEO of Delta Airlines; David Goode, Chairman/President/CEO of Norfolk Southern; and Thomas Donohue, President of the Chamber of Commerce of the United States of America. Also on my top list of fine servant leaders are P. S. Willmott, President and CEO of Zenith; Donald Schneider, President and CEO of Schneider National; and David Holmes, President of Reynolds and Reynolds. Many of my former partners at McKinsey & Company, Inc., did much to help me along the way. For all of them, let me sincerely thank Marvin Bower, who for so long was the forceful servant leader of McKinsey & Company, Inc. And let me thank several academics for their great help and encouragement over the years: Dr. John Langley of Tennessee and Dr. Douglas Lambert of Ohio State University. As an "athletic academic," let me thank Coach Gary Barnett of Northwestern University, who is both a great student and teacher of leadership. As a very special academic, let me thank Dean Donald P. Jacobs of the Kellogg Graduate School of Management at Northwestern University, who for the past twenty years has nurtured and inspired my academic career. Finally, I do want to thank three noble spirits who did so much to make the original publication of this book a physical reality: Marcia Lind, who typed and prepared the manuscript, and Michael Ward and Ken Landau of Visions Sports Management, who guided me during the final writing of the book.

To all of them (and many more) my grateful thanks and may God bless each of them always.

THE SERVANT LEADER

PRELUDE: "NEUSCHEL'S NUGGETS"

As a prelude to my book, I have crafted a series of "Thoughts for the Day" about various aspects of leadership. I offer these "nuggets" by way of introduction and, hopefully, inspiration.

1. It is not the lot of the leader to be served but rather his/her privilege to serve. *Ich Dien* appears prominently on the crest of the Prince of Wales: It says, so simply, "I serve." Putting this creed into action creates what I call the "servant leader." Plato in the fifth century B.C. gave us a credo that lays the basis for the "servant leader" when he said, "We govern for the benefit of the governed." I paraphrase that to say, "We lead for the benefit of the led."

2. The head is smart but not always wise. Perhaps the highest art in leadership is to balance the head—the seat of analysis and logic—and the heart—the seat of feeling and compassion. Understanding and practicing the appropriate balance is at the core of effective leadership. There is no book on how to balance the two. The balance depends on judgment and wisdom. This is one reason why leadership may be more art than science.

3. Effective leadership requires a high tolerance for ambiguity and learning to live and be productive in an increasingly uncertain environment. The managerial playing field will be messy, often disorderly, and continually changing. This will require a great deal of calm sorting out and striving to operate on an even keel in an ever-changing and churning sea. Inability to cope with uncertainty, constant change, disappointment, and even defeat as well as success is a stumbling

block to effective leadership. One important test of accomplished leadership is how well the leader copes with these uncertainties, these needs to change, as well as coping with both trials and successes.

4. The mature leader has:
   - A high flash point
   - A soft but strong and firm voice but rarely, if ever, needs to shout
   - Deep reserves of energy
   - Mental and emotional maturity
   - An inner peace and calmness that fosters stability in the face of tumult
   - A well-managed ego
   - Freedom from arrogance and moodiness
   - A keen sense of what really counts—an instinct for the essential

5. The leader needs more than integrity to be successful. But without integrity, and the trust it inspires, nothing else matters much.

6. The high-performing, trusted, and respected leader will have an unswerving sense of moral decency. Further, these traits will be perceived and believed by his/her followers.

7. An important undergirding for all managerial leadership—in fact, for all human achievement—is a deep and abiding desire for accomplishment, a burning desire to grow and perform at an ever higher level.

8. The effective manager/leader must have a capacity for abstraction, vision, and the ability to conceptualize. In addition, this requires the ability to translate the conceptual into

concrete specifics that are understood and meaningful to the people in the organization. This is the basis for translating vision into reality.

9. The successful leader energizes people as he/she leads them. The drive and energy of the leader must get reflected in the thoughts and actions of the people throughout the organization. The leader in fact must energize the people in the organization.

10. The effective leader is ever inspirationally dissatisfied and instills that feeling in the troops. It is a healthy kind of dissatisfaction that encourages reaching for higher levels of performance.

11. The leader needs vast amounts of physical, spiritual, and psychic energy. Frustrations, disappointments, and "high mountains" will drain away energy. The pressure to compete, to make changes, to face the new demands will be physically and emotionally tiring—it will be energy-draining and there is a continuing need to replenish the leader's fountain of energy.

12. Strong leaders do not nibble around the edges. They don't dabble with minutiae. Charles de Gaulle said it more poetically than I: "Be not like ordinary men who splash about in shallow water." You must move in (and be perceived to do so) and tackle the important issues where and when it counts.

13. Success in interpersonal relations does not depend on mental brilliance or a high IQ. It depends rather on practical intelligence, sensitivity, common sense, and emotional maturity, which is the sine qua non for successful relationships with others.

14. Courage is among the most desired of leadership qualities. Few will follow with enthusiasm the cowardly or the tentative leader. But remember, no amount of technique can produce

courage. Courage comes from the heart and the soul, and it can hardly be intellectualized.

15. The capacity to quickly identify and assess what is important is a quality common to successful executives. This quality is inherently part of a broader capacity and basic to solid, common sense (the source of judgment), which is an invaluable asset to the high performing leader.

16. Efforts to gain human understanding should dominate a leader's thinking and actions. The leader is neither a statistician nor an engineer. He/she is a leader of human beings operating in a world of Homo sapiens.

17. One significant test of quality leadership is how well the leader copes with disappointment, defeat, or some overriding adversity. Voltaire, in praising this quality in the Duke of Marlborough, called it "calm courage in the midst of tumult, that serenity of soul in danger." This is one of the greatest gifts of nature for command.

18. The meaningful image of the genuine leader is not just a surface picture at some instant in time. Rather, it is an honest reflection of the leader's values demonstrated over a period of time.

19. The leader needs unswerving strength of character. The choices will be difficult. The temptations will be many and difficult to resist. Making the right decisions will not be so much intellectual as demanding of one's character.

20. In the national football draft they still want to know how fast a player runs the forty-yard dash or the number of tackles made per game. But increasingly more attention is being devoted to a player's values, habits, personality, and ethics. There is a

strong message here as we evaluate the qualities of leaders. While both skill and character are vital, increasingly character will dominate.

21. It is a great leadership gift to have the naturalness of a child—to be straightforward, not artful, no acting, no pretense or guile. Naturalness and genuineness are priceless executive virtues.

22. The leader must be an extraordinary agent for change. In this world of rapid change and discontinuities, the leader must be out front to sense the need for change, to encourage change and growth, and to show the way for bringing it about. This capacity must be grounded in a keen sense of judgment and wisdom on what changes to make and how to bring them about. It takes tough, intelligent, and creative analysis, but the analysis must be "washed" with judgment and wisdom.

23. The leader must have the courage, the inner peace of mind and soul, and the will power to take difficult and sometimes very lonely positions.

24. Margaret Thatcher in her remarkable career has demonstrated many virtues which we admire. Foremost among them are constancy, determination, resoluteness, decisiveness, and, above all, sheer grit.

25. Stamina is the leader's ultimate resource. Little is much good without endurance. The capacity to "stay with it" and to keep coming back to the battle is a powerful leadership asset. This is evidenced by the ability to work long and hard, especially under pressure or carrying on effectively after disappointment. I recall a corporate president recently saying, "My greatest strength grows out of my tenacity." Life is more of a marathon than it is a dash.

26. You have to be able to say "yes" or "no" crisply. Don't waffle. You can withhold a decision for a more appropriate time. But do not be tentative in the process.

27. The effective leader is mentally and emotionally grown up. He/she has matured—is objective and forethoughtful. He/she is free of arrogance and moodiness and realistically well attuned to life. This leader exudes stability. Being an emotional yo-yo "turns off" followers.

28. The leader must never be haughty or mean or small. Arrogance after a breach of integrity is the cardinal leadership sin.

29. Effective leadership demands both stability and flexibility as well as a keen sense of reality. We do not move forward in nice even steps. It is start and stop, forward and backward, and even sideways. Through it all the leader must be capable of change but still remain anchored to the vision he/she has set before the organization. Like the captain of a ship who battles the sea and brings the ship back on course—so the leader guides the troops through the turbulence toward their goals, always being able to point the organization back to the target.

30. There is a strong need for commitment—not just compliance —to the organization and its vision. All high performing organizations have key leaders and subleaders imbued with deep commitment.

INTRODUCTION

The driving force behind the development of this book is my deep conviction that the future of the United States and the Free World depends upon their ability to develop the quality and quantity of leaders necessary to effectively manage and lead their institutions. I speak of thousands of institutions, large and small, that proliferate in our society. We are a society of organizations. Indeed, it has been mankind's ability, particularly in the Free World, to get important tasks done through people in an organization that has been the driving force behind the success of industrialized and highly productive societies. This has been one of the important ingredients in the awesome rise of America's industrial power. In the decades leading up to World War II and in the fifty plus years following, America performed an industrial miracle. We won the most massive world conflict and then helped to rebuild Japan and Western Europe. Underlying this was our remarkable ability to manage and lead.

As we move through the last decade of this century the scene has changed. America is no longer solely the clear world leader. Japan and Germany are challenging our economic strength. In some ways Japan has overtaken us. In the automobile, banking, steel, and electronics industries, Japan is outdoing us in head-to-head competition. My purpose here is not to examine the reasons why Japan is outperforming the United States on a number of economic fronts. Probably the causes are many and, in combination, very complex. One cause, often cited, is the lagging productivity of our work force compared with that of Japan. Perhaps. I think it is broader and deeper than simply worker productivity. I strongly suspect that there has been a weakening in the fabric of the management and leadership of our industrial organizations. And I believe these shortcomings in leadership are equally prevalent in the other sectors of our society, such as government, universities, hospitals, and churches. A few examples in the industrial sector illustrate my point. Twenty years ago, our automobile industry dominated the world markets. One has to ask the question: where was the General Motors (or Ford or Chrysler) board of directors and senior management during the years when the Japanese industry made its assault on our markets? There have been many theories and explanations offered. The fact remains: at the start of this competitive onslaught, the American automobile industry was standing in the dominant position in the world. While there may be other contributing factors, we have to finally focus in on one irrefutable fact: the Japanese industry out-managed and out-led its American counterpart.

We can ask similar questions about industrial companies and former giants such as Pan American, TWA, or International Harvester. Pan American was once the premier airline in the world. Trans World Airlines also was a dominant, well-managed airline, and International Harvester was the world leader in both farm equipment and truck manufacturing and marketing. Over a period of ten to fifteen years, each eroded and lost the competitive battle in world markets. Why? Long term, the board of directors and senior management must be charged with the responsibility for the lack of enduring competitive strength of each of these enterprises.

As a final illustration we can point to the steel industry. From a position of world dominance following World War II the industry eroded away, clearly beaten in world markets. Perhaps it was the victim of its own success in the boom years of the 1940s and 1950s. The fact remains that the boards of directors and senior managements of our steel companies for ten to fifteen years presided over a gradual decline of this industry. Fortunately, it is beginning to revive. But unfortunately, the quality of its managerial leadership eroded over a long period of time.

To repeat an earlier point, this kind of leadership erosion is occurring in other sectors of our society. Why is this? What is going on here? Let me offer a hypothesis. First, over all I believe we are still world leaders in technology. Not perhaps in every phase of technology, but on balance we still are Number One. If we have any problem here it is that our technology has outpaced our ability to manage and lead it. To put it another way, our problem is in the conversion of technology into product, not in the technology itself. Also I have no quarrel with our marketing, organizational, and financial acumen.

My hypothesis is this. Our leadership is experiencing a diminution in ethics, a loss of enduring values. These weakening factors are exacerbated by a preoccupation with the short term. We seem to have a cancerous malaise that has been fostered by greed, selfishness, and the desire to get it big and get it quick. We are more concerned about achieving quick shareholder values than building an enduring organization that can increase its capacity to produce useful products or services more competitively and more effectively on an enduring basis. Our mania for takeovers and leveraged buyouts in the 1980s is further evidence of our desire for immediate gain, our eagerness to manipulate the deal rather than engage in long-term building. John Bryan of Sara Lee (a well-managed company) recently expressed it well when he wrote, "I grew up with the notion that you build, grow, and develop rather than pile on debt, strip it down, and take your chances."

If my hypothesis is correct, it raises a straightforward question. What steps might we take to revitalize the quality and strength of our leadership? In brief, how can we put more character into the way we lead? What I will suggest is not a "how to" list. Rather, I want to outline what I believe are the major changes we must bring about.

In the chapters of this book I shall discuss more specifically the anatomy of effective, quality leadership. Here are some major changes to consider.

1. Reestablish and revitalize the concept that the highest calling of leadership is to lead for the benefit of the led. This calls forth a concept taught by Plato twenty-four hunderd years ago. It is the only type of leadership that has enduring significance—a type of leadership that builds toward long-term values of the total community.

2. Avoid the short-term drive for gains that grows out of our excessive greed. This is based on the thesis that the highest purpose of any organization—industrial, commercial, or eleemosynary —is to provide society with a beneficial product or service on

an enduring basis. This demands that leadership build an enterprise's capacity to produce, to serve, and to better society. This would preclude the quick manipulation that benefits a few and, most importantly, manipulations that may diminish the capacity of the enterprise to build and serve for the long term.

3. Seek the qualities of the servant leader. The servant leader by my definition leads people in a manner that helps them grow and increase their capacity to contribute (useful products and services) and in the process gain the satisfaction of making a greater contribution to the success of the organization.

4. Lead with an unswerving dedication to the highest level of ethics. In our American tradition this means unquestioned observance of the Judeo-Christian principles. Other cultures too have codes of ethics based on their religious faiths.

5. Ensure that the driving purpose of the enterprise is to provide high quality, useful products of genuine value to society and in the process to realize profits in order to maintain the organization on a healthy, competitive basis.

If all this sounds too Pollyannaish, then we are in real trouble. It is imperative in a free market society that an atmosphere of trust permeate our business and government actions. When this trust breaks down —as it has been doing—we get constricting, sometimes misguided, legislation that can inhibit our capacity as a nation to be productive. Such deviant behavior fosters little but more distrust. As government and business leaders fail to live up to these high ethical standards, it suggests to followers that they can do the same. It is a two-way street—we follow as we lead and lead as we follow.

In the chapters that follow I shall explore the anatomy of leadership in a way, I believe, that will help managers and leaders to rethink who they are and how they should be leading. My objective is to provoke the leader to examine his/her capacity to be a servant leader—to lead in ways that will result in more enduring value to their organizations and in the process to our economy and the larger society.

1 PUTTING LEADERSHIP INTO PERSPECTIVE

There are no simple formulas that can guarantee success as a leader. There are no slick, prepackaged techniques that can teach you to lead or manage in a matter of hours. Leadership is a skill that requires capacity, dedication, and experience (which means time to live and learn). Therefore, in this book I will deal with fundamental values and ideas about leadership. The book will deal with many of the enduring aspects of leadership, covering the fundamentals, the old-fashioned but essential "blocking and tackling."

My views on leadership have been shaped by some fifty years of experience. Early on, I spent five years observing and practicing the art of leadership as an officer in the U.S. Army both in the United States and in the Pacific Theater during World War II. Then I spent over thirty years with McKinsey & Company, Inc., the international management consulting firm, where I served industrial and government clients on all six continents. The focus of that work was primarily in strategic planning, organization structure, management development, and logistics. After retiring from McKinsey & Company in 1979, I became a professor of corporate governance at Northwestern University's J. L. Kellogg Graduate School of Management. I also served during this period for twelve years as managing director of the Transportation Center at Northwestern, which is one of the leading institutions for research and education on transportation and logistics in the United States and perhaps the world.

Despite my academic involvement, this book will not be an academic treatise. I will not, in fact cannot, support many of the conclusions I reach about leadership with an array of evidence from scholarly studies.

I am writing this book because I am convinced that the greatest challenge facing the Free World's societies today is developing a sufficient number of quality leaders to lead our institutions. I am further convinced that increasing human effectiveness is one of the few remaining business frontiers, mastery of which will give a competitive advantage to our corporations in the future. It also will be important to our universities, our churches, our government—any organization. Clearly the individual who aspires to be an effective leader has most to gain from meeting the challenge of increasing the effectiveness of those who work with him or her.

Therefore, the purpose of this book is to provoke, inform, and inspire those who desire to increase their capacity to manage and lead. It is not meant to be a study of organization behavior, rather it will focus on the individual as leader. I intend to explore the anatomy of leadership, to dissect it and examine many of its important facets. I wish to add some light to a subject pondered by humanity throughout the ages. My hope is that this book will serve to enhance the practices of successful executives and to serve as a supplement to aspiring business students at the university level.

The trend toward teaching leadership at both graduate and undergraduate levels in our universities is a strong one that will increase in importance in the future. Not that leadership can be taught in the classroom. Basically we learn to lead by leading. But we can learn much in the classroom that can serve as a guide to shaping and developing our own leadership patterns.

During my thirty years at McKinsey I had frequent opportunities to work on client studies with graduates from most of the major graduate business schools. It is true that because of our rigorous selection process we recruited the "Best of the Best." Perhaps therefore my exposure did not necessarily represent a universal pattern. However, I did have considerable exposure to MBAs from such graduate schools as Harvard, Dartmouth, Carnegie Mellon, Chicago, Wharton, Stanford, and of course, Kellogg—to name a few. I was overall most favorably impressed with their maturity and solid understanding of what constituted quality leadership as we observed and studied it in client organizations. Based on much personal exposure to their client work and many one-on-one in-depth conversations, I sensed that their

MBA experience helped them to distinguish and evaluate quality leadership as they were to later observe it in client executives themselves. While they clearly were skilled at analysis and the numbers, I sensed that they had also acquired the beginnings of wisdom along the way. Obviously during my twenty years on the Kellogg faculty I have seen the transformation that takes place during students' two years in the MBA program. Admittedly they do not manage or lead an organization in their two years in Kellogg. But I am convinced that the typical MBA graduate is well positioned and motivated to assume a managerial leadership role in their after school business experience.

While talking about Kellogg, it is important to highlight the leadership contribution of Donald Jacobs, the long time Dean of the Kellogg School. In his leadership he practices the philosophy of Jethro, the teacher of Moses. Dean Jacobs has perfected the fine art of delegation with great skill while in the process he mentors, develops, and grows the faculty. This has a cascading, energizing impact on the MBA students. The students clearly recognize that the faculty is encouraged—yes, charged—to grow and reach and stretch. This is indeed a form of servant leadership that Donald Jacobs practices, one in which the faculty is coached and challenged to make an increasing contribution to the quality of teaching and thus to help the students and the school to grow; and in the process, the faculty has grown and blossomed and as a result gains great personal satisfaction because of the increased contribution they are able to make to the success of the school. This is servant leadership as practiced in academia.

One important element that university training can contribute to the aspiring leader is a well-rounded view of the world and the student's place in it. While leaders must be competent in their field, they must never believe the sun rises and sets only on their own function or area of management. Nor should leaders view themselves solely as technical experts—leaders solve problems through people in an organization. We are faced with a nagging, perennial problem. Technology outpaces our ability to manage it. Thus our future progress depends more on our ability to lead with better technology, not just to create technology. The sine qua non of leadership is to recognize that accomplishments can be made only through your people.

People are the primary materials with which leaders work, and the leader's task is to organize and inspire them to achieve the mission. Technique and process are not enough. Great skills in finance, computer logic, or marketing, to name a few, are of little value unless we have the capacity to use them to get important things done through people. It is vital to understand that the individual's function is part of a living whole, to understand how each role fits in, how the various roles supplement or even conflict with the other parts or people in the business. It is necessary to know what are reasonable and realistic trade-offs that can and should be made with other areas of the total activity. The highest calling of leaders is to know how to shape the parts to make them fit better into the whole. Just as John Donne spoke of mankind when he said, "No man is an island, entire of itself; every man is a piece of the continent," so it is with individual leaders at any level in the organization. The leader is part of the whole and his or her responsibility is to make the whole greater because of his/her leadership presence.

We are all aware that much already has been written on the subject of leadership. Authors have expounded on the subject since the earliest of times. You may recall that Jethro gave Moses a great fatherly lecture on leadership that helped save the Israelite nation almost thirty-four hundred years ago. Along the way other great minds have thought and written about leadership. For example:

- More than four hundred years before Christ, Plato (428–348 B.C.) analyzed the ways of rulers with marvelous insights in his *Republic,* in which he speaks of the ideal state or republic where philosopher-rulers would be supreme and they would "rule to enhance the ruled."
- In the first century A.D., Plutarch wrote brilliantly about the lives of Roman and Greek leaders. His biographies of Fabius, Alexander, Caesar, Anthony, and Marcellus, for example, pro-

vide us with some of the finest and most insightful lessons on leadership found anywhere in literature.

- Shakespeare, in the sixteenth century, had much wisdom on the subject. He often borrowed from Plutarch and the Bible, but re-expressed their thoughts in unusually penetrating and beautiful ways. His studies of the struggle of a Hamlet, a Macbeth, a King Lear, or a Caesar are unforgettable examples of leadership under stress.
- In the Middle Ages, Machiavelli gave us much food for thought in his brilliant and incisive writing about how princes get, hold, and use power.
- More recently, the elitist French leader Charles de Gaulle said, "Men are of no importance. What counts is who commands."

James MacGregor Burns, one of the leading contemporary writers on the subject, says, "Leadership is a baffling subject." He maintains that he is still groping to understand the nature of leadership, and adds, "It is one of the most observed and least understood human phenomena on earth."

Burns is correct. Ironically, more has been written and less understood about leadership than almost any other topic in the field of behavioral science. I had the privilege of meeting at length with Jim Casey, the founder, one of the early leaders, and the driving force behind the success of United Parcel Service. I became acquainted with him during his later years as an elder statesman. At that time he spoke from a well of wisdom. He expressed the strong belief that only one thing could ever drive UPS out of business and that would be if it were to lose its inspired leadership, from its drivers through all levels of management up to the chief executive officer.

Leadership is more art than science. No human being can be accurately and unequivocally categorized. My approach, therefore, will be to:

- Convey some lessons about leadership I have observed in business, military, church, hospital, and university organizations.

- Examine the important responsibilities of the leader.
- Evaluate the significant traits of leaders. What are they like and what do they have in common?
- Extract lessons from the experiences of leaders selected from a wide variety of organizations.

When you finish reading this book, you will not be a better manager or leader. I repeat, you can learn to lead only by leading. But the book will help in a small way to push you along in your leadership journey and show you how to make the most of it. It will do so more readily if, as you read and study the pages that follow, you will ask yourself, and ponder, the following questions:

- Have I moved closer to my mission? In fact, do I have a mission? Has it been clearly articulated and accepted? Do I really live my mission?
- How good a leader have I been? What specific improvements in the people for whom I am responsible have I brought about in the past year—few years? In what ways have I elevated my organization? How is it better because of me?
- What standards of measurement have I set for myself? What constitutes improvement? What am I shooting for as a leader? In fact, what does a good leader do—what separates him/her from the ordinary?
- Have I thought deeply and in an organized way about the jobs of my subordinates, that is, what must they do, and how, to be successful—to grow? How can I help them?
- Do I know how each of my subordinates really is performing— where each needs guidance, inspiration, or technical assistance? Does each understand the enterprise and live our mission—do they know what I want and how I will judge them?
- How am I perceived by my subordinates and to what extent am I truly being followed? If I did not have the badge of office, to what extent would I be looked upon as a natural leader?
- How well have I ordered my priorities? Where and how can I

make the most difference? Am I targeting in on the right places? The right activities? The right people?

○ How many people for whose performance I am responsible could handle my job in six months—in two years?

○ Who has truly grown under me and what role did I play in that growth?

Far more important than what is written here is what you the reader think, particularly about those provocative questions. You must learn to think deeply about your own role as a leader, the quality of your leadership, and how you can improve. Critical in this process is reflection on how well or poorly you have led in the past. One must understand and learn from one's own past in order to improve future performance. I hope the questions listed above will act as a stimulus and a challenge. Take a moment right now to think about them. Only as you take specific action on these questions will any of what is written here have any value to you.

Before wading into deeper waters, let me set a bit more perspective by pointing out some important reasons why all of us should be increasingly concerned about managerial leadership.

The management task in our society is becoming increasingly complex and difficult. Our deregulated and highly competitive business environment places a premium on quality management and leadership, more so than at any time in the past. The globalization of world markets has intensified competition and raised the demands for success. As a result there will be more managerial obsolescence in our organizations in the future. Moreover, people in our organizations today raise questions. They want to know why. Many workers today do not know "their place." They are smarter and better informed. We no longer have servants or slaves. Their approach is not servile but competitive and adversarial. This undoubtedly makes the leader's role more difficult, at least more challenging.

Let us turn now to look at managing and leading from a global point of view. We are a society of organizations in which there is much distrust and many possible dangers. Many fear:

- Nuclear war—an atomic holocaust;
- Worldwide epidemics—like a replay of the black plague, or even our new fear of the spread of AIDS;
- Widespread famine such as was experienced in sub–Saharan Africa some years ago and in northeast Africa in recent times.

Personally, I fear even more the likelihood of a general failure to develop leaders of high quality in sufficient numbers to effectively manage our institutions—at all levels, from the grassroots manager to the president. We are a society of organizations; we get things done through people in an organized way. Humankind has progressed because of the ability to work effectively in organizations. The demand for new, quality managers is never-ending—it is insatiable. We must never stop developing new leaders.

Some years ago while on a consulting assignment in Caracas, I had occasion to meet with a senior official in the Venezuelan government. After our business was completed he shared with me many interesting observations about his country and its struggle to improve its economic strength and the well-being of its people. He told me that Venezuela was using its oil revenue to build industrial facilities to help bootstrap the country into the twenty-first century as an industrialized nation. He went on to say that they had built petroleum refineries, chemical plants, and cement plants, to mention a few. And with great sadness he said they were not able to run these new plants effectively or economically because they did not have a sufficient number of quality leaders at the foreman, supervisor, and other middle-management levels, as well as in some more senior positions. That conversation drove home to me most forcefully the great need of an industrial society for managers who can lead at all levels up and down its organizations. We could always use another Churchill, or a Bismarck, or a George Washington. But equally or perhaps even more important are less lofty needs—for effective leaders at all levels throughout our organizations. In fact, I am convinced that in our preoccupation with leadership at the presidential level we might be undervaluing leadership at the middle and lower levels—at the "front line." Only through building top-to-bottom leadership can we create a culture in which people will work together cooperatively, productively, and humanely.

In a recent speech at Northwestern University, Carol Presley, the former senior vice president of Federal Express, expressed a powerful truth about leadership and its importance. She said, "You can't survive in Federal Express if you can't lead people." Anyone who wants to make a difference in that company will make it through exercising quality leadership. As I have pointed out, more is expected of the individual leader today than ever before. Many cannot cope with the higher demands of our increasingly competitive society. Many cannot handle the increased competition and stress. Therefore, the rate of managerial obsolescence is high. The great burden on corporate leaders is to create a climate that will enable a large percentage of existing leaders to grow and learn not only to cope with change but to create the changes needed to compete in highly competitive, market-driven world trade.

Here is a cautionary tale about a company that is struggling and sputtering with inadequate leadership. Just a few years before our true story begins, the former president was removed because of a strategic marketing blunder that resulted in a loss of confidence by the board. There followed a period of floundering; the company did not seem to know where it was going. Middle managers were restless because they did not see a clear path ahead. They wanted a leader to rally around. When the current president was brought in from the outside, he was represented to be a quality leader who could chart a firm course. However, after several months, executives within the company began expressing disappointment in the new president's leadership performance. They had hoped for a steady, bright star to follow. Instead they had a leader who did not seem to understand the organization's critical need for a sense of steady, focused direction. They were not sure where he wanted to take them. It is important to note his shortcomings because they are not uncommon. Whether true in fact or not, his people perceived that he exhibited at least the following significant shortcomings.

1. This new leader is not accessible to his people. He is too remote and executives have to either wait too long for his review and decision or else go ahead and act, taking the chance that they might be wrong and have to pay the penalty.
2. He does not practice what he preaches. He demands cost reduction and containment from the organization but exceeds his own budget. He is perceived to be a heavy spender. He fails to lead by example.
3. Finally, his people sincerely feel that he is not leading them anywhere. He has given no clear direction—they are not sure where he wants to take them.

This calls to mind the admonition almost two thousand years ago of St. Paul to the Corinthians, "If the sound of the trumpet is unclear who will prepare for battle?"

1. *Be accessible.* Subleaders, in all organizations and particularly in a foundering one, need to feel their top leaders are available to them. It is from accessibility that they draw confidence and a greater sense of being a closer part of the team. Expressed another way, leaders influence and motivate by their *presence.* Particularly when there are problems or challenges, it is imperative that the leaders be present. The leader must bring two things to any crisis or tough situation: (a) a perceived willingness to take the heat, that he/she will not duck taking the "gaff," and (b) a sense of calmness, that he/she can work out with his/her team an effective solution. One cannot lead in absentia.
2. *Be consistent in word and deed.* This is a more sophisticated way of saying "lead by example." Here is an interesting recent case in point. Early in December 1988, Lou Holtz, Notre Dame football coach, banned two of his star players from playing in the most important game of the year, for the No. 1 ranking, against Southern California. Lou Holtz had set strict rules and they were disobeyed. His willingness to live his prin-

ciples even at high personal cost did much to enhance his image as a leader with his team and the whole sports world.

3. *Set a clear course.* The first task of leadership is to articulate the mission and support efforts to achieve it. There has to be a sense of confidence among the followers (the subleaders) that senior leaders (and subleaders) know where they are going. This is not to suggest that an organization must, or can, move in a straight path directly to each goal. In fact, running a company is like steering a ship on a rough sea; it requires a strong hand at the helm. The ship may be forced off course by tides and wind but the helmsman rights the ship and keeps returning to its intended course. The crew needs to be assured that the captain will keep their craft, the organization, on course.

Assuredly, the quality of leadership varies significantly from organization to organization. In each industry, I suspect, you will find a few companies that are extremely well run, some whose leadership is mediocre, and others that are poorly led. Over time, the difference in performance of leaders within any one company is likely to be equally wide. *This insight has led me to believe that quality leadership, which can unleash the power of people in the organization, is the enduring ingredient that will enable one organization to out-perform competition.*

More than fifty years ago, Albert Einstein addressed the subject of scientific management with these profound words: "It is not enough that you should understand about applied science in order that your work may increase man's blessings. Concern for man himself and his fate must always form the chief interest of all technical endeavors in order that the creations of our minds shall be a blessing and not a curse to mankind. Never forget this in the midst of your diagrams and equations."

There is an old Chinese proverb that goes something like this: "If you are planning for one year, grow rice—if for twenty years, plant trees. If you are planning for centuries, grow men." So it is with our organizations. We must teach the leaders how to teach and grow new leaders at every level within the organization. Only in this way can the immense power that lies within any group be unleashed—the power of people, the power of subleaders, down and throughout the organization.

2   TWO REQUIREMENTS OF THE SUCCESSFUL EXECUTIVE

You need at least two qualities and capacities to be a successful manager/leader of a business or, in fact, any type of organization. These two essentials are:

○ A high degree of business and organizational smarts.
○ The capacity to provide inspired leadership.

Let me cite a military analogy to emphasize how vital each is and how the two essentials complement each other. During combat it requires truly inspired leadership to take a company of soldiers up an open hill under withering enemy fire to capture the hilltop. Indeed it does. But it is a tragedy if the officer leads the soldiers up the wrong (unimportant, nonessential) hill. Clearly, in any organization, the leaders must inspire the people to climb up many difficult hills, but most if not all the time the leader must pick the right hills to climb.

The purposes of this book will be to deal primarily with inspired leadership. But I want to take a few minutes in this chapter to discuss what I mean by business and organizational smarts. Here are a few examples of what I have in mind.

1. The capacity to think strategically as well as tactically. The ability to move freely from the pragmatic to the conceptual and back. This is vital if the leader is to convert creative ideas into realistic implementation.

2. The capacity to identify the key factors for success in any business or organization as a whole and for each important segment of the enterprise. This means sensing where the leverage is in order to discern what few things are important and where you should focus your efforts. Part of business smarts

is the capacity to identify the few essential factors and the discipline to focus on them.

3. Knowledge of the product, the marketplace, and the key competitive players in the business. Red Auerbach, now president of the Boston Celtics, was for years the coach who led them to become one of the all-time great sports franchises in America. Red Auerbach was asked some years ago why he did not take over the historically great but, at the time, floundering Boston Red Sox baseball team. After some thought he said, "No," because he had too little feel for the product or the marketplace. He felt he had a "sixth sense" about what made a great basketball player, and he could quickly judge this greatness. He lacked that knowledge and instinct about baseball and baseball players and the baseball fan.

4. Intellectual and psychological capacity to drive toward low cost. This is critical to support a sound strategy. There is a compelling need to be the low cost producer in our free market society.

5. A good sense of the cost/profit economics of your business. In a recent talk I heard, the speaker told about the late Sam Walton's simple strategy for business success. Walton said, "I always have a big number at the end of the month to subtract from." While he was being purposely oversimplistic to drive home his point, Sam Walton had a unique and very clear concept of the proper relationship between cost and revenue.

6. Having a sense of interrelatedness. This means the capacity to see the interrelationships of the parts to the whole, that is, visualizing how each piece of the enterprise adds strength to and gains strength from the entire organization.

7. Finally, one of the greatest of executive gifts is a sense of what will fly and what will not, that is, a "good belly" for the business. There is not enough time, energy, or resources to try everything. The successful executive will have an innate sense of what will work, what will not.

Having these business and organizational smarts is critical. After all, you must lead your troops up the right hills. But the other part of the equation is that through inspired leadership you must lead your people up whatever hill you believe is important to climb and "take it." This book of course is about the inspired leadership component of the equation. However, I did want at least to touch on the business smarts part of the equation. Therefore, I will now turn my attention fully to inspired leadership, the main focus of this book.

I am deeply convinced that the last frontier open to us—open to any organization, open to any individual executive—is to increase human effectiveness. That is the essential. Let me approach the issue of increasing human effectiveness by exploring the anatomy of inspired leadership.

In years past, there has been increasing concern among business writers and some scholars that our graduate business schools are developing managers, not leaders. Certainly there is a difference between the roles of manager and leader, as writers like Warren Bennis, James MacGregor Burns, and Abraham Zaleznik, who are among today's leading scholars on leadership, have pointed out in detail. Yes, managers and leaders are different; and it is important to recognize the difference.

While scholars have made some profound distinctions, it may also be helpful at the outset to examine the definitions found in Webster's unabridged dictionary.

Manager: "One who conducts business affairs with economy—with efficiency." (James MacGregor Burns would describe this role as transactional, that is, carrying out the business at hand under the existing general framework.)

Leader: "One who goes before to guide or show the way. The foremost person in an advancing body. The one who has followers." (Burns refers to this role as transforming because it may involve moving in a different direction or changing the culture or method of operation.)

The lament usually attached to the accusation that business schools are developing managers is that businesses are too often run by managers and not leaders. This often suggests or at least leaves the impression that managers are the "not-so-good guys" and leaders the "good guys." Warren Bennis goes so far as to assert that one of the differences between managers and leaders is that the manager does things right but the leader does the right things. Such critiques, in my opinion, miss the point, and in the process, unfortunately, they seem to belittle the role of the manager. *In fact, the roles of both the manager and the leader are critical.* The point is that successful organizations are run by men and women who are in combination *both* managers and leaders. All of us possess some of the qualities of each. The problem is not in deciding which to be, but rather in achieving the right balance of the managerial and leadership characteristics that each individual executive should possess. The position of the individual and his/her responsibilities for the affairs of the enterprise will of course determine what the appropriate balance should be. I can state categorically that no successful executive with whom I have worked or who I have observed professionally during the past forty-five years was solely a manager or exclusively a leader. All applied some combination of traits—manager and leader—in carrying out their executive duties. This experience convinced me that it is rather naive and simplistic to think of managers and leaders as requiring a totally separate and distinctively different set of attributes. It is, however, a tempting notion because the task of defining the proper blend of managerial and leadership traits for a given position is incredibly complex. In most jobs, the lines of distinction between the roles of the leader and manager are blurred and overlapping. And to further complicate matters, the great majority of people possess more of one set of traits than the other, sometimes in the wrong proportions for the job at hand.

Many approaches to management development tend to separate managerial traits from those of leadership. This is unfortunate since both are vital in the makeup of a complete, effective executive.

Why were General George S. Patton's men willing to go through battle for him? Because he was a splendid tactician (manager). But that is only part of the reason. Patton possessed a kind of energizing bravado that stirred men into action. His presence inspired them with the belief that if they followed him, they would achieve victory. Such a balance of traits is just as important for the business executive. He or she must be competent in the substance of the job, possess the motivational spark (or charisma) that will inspire others, and have a sense of organization to make it all come off. These characteristics—competence, charisma, and organization—are combined in effective executives, whom I call manager/leaders.

I use the term manager/leader to describe the effective executive in any organization. I also use the term managerial leadership to bridge the two vital concepts. As we move through the 1990s and into the twenty-first century, changes in business organizations are necessary due to deregulation, growing diversity, tougher competition, and globalization. Leadership is needed to provide the vision and create the positive attitude and organizational sense of courage to make changes. However, it takes solid managerial attention, skills, and follow-up to organize the pieces and make them work. *Both qualities, manager and leader, are fundamental and vital. Too much vision with little implementing action gets us nowhere. Too much implementing action and little vision may get us to the wrong place.*

An interesting acknowledgment of the phenomenon I call the manager/leader occurred while I was serving on the compensation committee of a corporate board during a critical time in this company's history. We were considering the issue of succession to the presidency. In discussing two candidates for his job, the president and CEO who was soon to retire commented that "one of the candidates is more leader than manager, the other more manager than leader." He concluded that at the company's point in its history the executive who was more leader than manager would make the better president.

Clearly the president of the enterprise should be heavily endowed with leadership talents. The heads of the marketing and accounting departments need considerable managerial skills. But those executives also need leadership qualities as well as the talents of a manager. In fact, as I stated earlier, every successful executive I have worked with or observed in the last four decades possessed some combination of both traits.

Recognizing the existence of the manager/leader is an important step. Doing so clears the air of scholarly nitpicking and puts in better perspective wrongheaded views such as those expressed by the former U.S. Secretary of Health, Education and Welfare, John Gardner, when he observed that America was raising a generation of managers, not leaders.

But it is only the first step. We then must consider what balance of managerial and leadership traits an executive should have for a given job. Discerning and understanding this balance is the real art of selecting executive talent and of training oneself for a position. The balance of this book will concentrate on how to cultivate such discernment and understanding.

The leader needs unswerving strength of character. The choices will be difficult, the temptations many. Making the right decisions will not be so much intellectual as demanding of one's character and judgment.

The image of the leader is not his superficial self but rather the sum total of a system of values demonstrated over time. When this manifestation is clear and consistent and reflects a quality of personal integrity, it is a powerful instrument. Integrity implies that a person has developed over time a consistent ordering of a system of values, attitudes, and goals.

Fundamental traits of personality and depth of character are more vital than intelligence in a leader. Intelligence by itself is not the strongest factor that motivates people to follow. It is the qualitative appeal of such characteristics as integrity, maturity, consistency, enthusiasm, and perseverance that makes people fall in line behind a leader. To oversimplify, leadership is leading people, and the sort of talent in interpersonal relations that leadership requires does not depend solely on intellectual endowment.

The results of studies of the relationship between IQ levels and leadership suggest that there is little positive correlation. This is not to say that a brilliant person could not be a leader, nor am I suggesting that we want an unintelligent person as a leader. But I am saying that intelligence alone will not a leader make; in fact, it is just one of many requirements.

A leader's character and personality are often demonstrated in seemingly small ways. Two examples of this come to mind. One was when President Ronald Reagan was shot early in his first term of office. Despite the severity of his wounds, he retained his composure and joked with his surgeons when he arrived at the hospital, saying he hoped they were all good Republicans. His calmness and coolness under duress was a great tonic to the hospital staff, who had visions of a repeat of the Kennedy tragedy in Dallas. Reagan's attitude during that incident did much to demonstrate the mark of a man—one who could be calm and "manly" under conditions of adversity and distress. It went a long way toward establishing the positive leadership image he built during his first term.

The second example is Pope John Paul II. His robust personality, his smile, his strong but gentle face, and his continual willingness to travel among the people have made him one of the most admired and loved leaders in the world.

Both of these men were intelligent. Both possessed considerable wisdom. But neither reached the pinnacle of leadership as a result of intellectual acumen. Intelligence is not the major ingredient that set them apart from other men. Their leadership ability definitely emanated from strong traits of character and personality.

Business executives, specifically, do not show a strong correlation between leadership and IQ test scores. These manager/leaders have what can be described as a practical intelligence that enables them to:

- Relate the individual parts to the whole
- Balance the short and long term
- Possess an innate sense of when to discuss and when to act
- Judge when to persevere and when to acquiesce
- Think in multidimensional terms
- Understand other points of view
- Have an innate sense of what "will fly" and what will not

I am not saying that people want unintelligent leaders or that our manager/leaders are not smart. My point is simply that the traits that cause a person to stand out as a leader in a group are usually such qualities as strength of character, a strong sense of values, or some other dominant or unusual element of personality. In any group of reasonably intelligent people a leader or leaders will emerge because he or she possesses desirable strength of character and personality and not because of intellectual capacity or some intelligence quotient.

Harold Ganeen, the former chairman of ITT, said recently that *"honesty is at the very heart of good management."* I agree with him 100 percent. I would add that integrity is at the core of all voluntary leadership and followership. To be sure, honesty and trust alone do not add up to leadership ability. The successful leader needs much more. But unless there is a strong element of trust among the followers, there cannot be effective leadership. Expressed simply, without trust and integrity nothing else matters much. People would rather follow a trustworthy plodder than a genius who may be short on integrity and fails to understand people and how to motivate them.

Yes, character and personality are the foundations of leadership ability.

Leadership is more judgment than knowledge, more art than science, more human relations than savvy. This is why it cannot be learned like a formula or conferred like a title.

Remember that leadership and followership represent a continuum. Followership sets the pattern for leadership. The leader cannot cheat up and get trust from below. The leader's own style of followership provides the model for his/her own people to imitate.

All leaders are also followers. Everyone must answer to some higher leader or authority. This paradoxical truth raises some questions. What is the relationship between followership and leadership? How does one's role as a follower affect his/her leadership? What effect does the way a leader follows have on subordinates?

Aristotle long ago summed up a significant share of the answer to those questions in a sentence: "He who has never learned to obey cannot be a good commander."

Followership precedes and evolves into leadership. There is a great church hymn written back in 1839 whose words have a poignant, relevant message: "O lead me, Lord, that I may lead." The clear though unstated message here is that the way we are led (as followers) will have great impact or how we in turn lead. It is also a great truth that quality leadership from above enables a leader to provide in turn a higher quality of leadership down through the organization.

There is a need to imbue followership with intelligence, courage, and committed support.

○ *Intelligence.* In following, you offer intelligent ideas to your leaders in order to enhance the operation.
○ *Courage.* The will to disagree—without confrontation—and to

express strongly felt convictions that may not be popular.

○ *Loyalty.* Despite honest disagreements, in the end you remain loyal and supportive—or leave.

The same trust and commitment you offer to your leader sets the stage for the kind of trust and followership you elicit when you, in turn, lead those below you. You cannot cheat those above and expect respect from those below. In the hierarchy of an organization, your followers will watch carefully how you yourself follow. So as a follower you will set the pattern of your leadership and the standard of quality you will demand. You also determine as a follower how your followers will one day follow you. As you understand and develop the art of followership, you increase your own capacity to lead wisely.

It is important to study the anatomy of followership—that is, why people follow. The reasons can range all the way from pure fear to an exalted sense that following a specific leader will result in success and satisfaction.

But let's begin by examining more specifically how a leader builds and gains support.

1. The first and most important source of support is achieving a history of successful performance. The department head, company president, or dean of a school whose operations are being carried out in a successful style is per se in a strong position. Few presidents whose companies are doing well are removed from office. The manager/leader simply draws strength and organizational support when his/her operations are perceived to be functioning successfully. Conversely, poor performance of the company, department, or unit opens the manager/leader up to questions and often can result in criticism even beyond the performance of the organization itself. Other quarrels or dissatisfactions may surface during periods of low performance by the organization. This will be more likely to occur—in fact, be magnified—if the manager/leader is not personally

liked by the organization.

2. Secondly, the manager/leader can draw power from a loyal, strong management group. Such a group is particularly important during periods of adversity—when overall performance may be down or when a particularly tough challenge faces the organization. When a management group closes ranks to carry out the tough tasks required in a crisis, it gives the leader a great source of power. This kind of support can do much to give comfort to a board of directors during periods of low performance.

3. A third and final source of support is the board of directors itself. The board is the ultimate source of power for the president and senior officers. A strong sense of confidence in the members of senior management by the directors both collectively and on an individual basis is vital to effective managerial leadership. This confidence is based on the belief that the manager/leader(s) can indeed perform. It requires a feeling of total trust that the manager/leader is and will be totally open and honest with the board. We will see in a later chapter why integrity and trust (assuming competence) are the foundation stones for building strong, enduring leadership.

Clearly, manager/leaders must work at getting support up, down, and across—wherever in the organization it can be found. They also must build followership by example, in the way they live and comport themselves.

Leaders get support because they give support to others. This idea may prove slippery, but it is important to grasp and use. Trust begets trust. By believing in people, you increase the possibility that others will believe in you. So it is with support. By building the troops they in turn are motivated to build.

The raison d'etre of effective leadership and followership is to generate strong loyalty in all directions—up, down, and across. Unfortunately, the importance to leaders of exhibiting a sense of loyalty to those whom they themselves follow is often overlooked. The esteem of peers and followers can be the salvation of the leader in times of stress and uncertainty. Too often ambitious executives look only "up" for support. In the process they forget care and concern for those they work with and those on levels below them. *Support from followers is critical to achieving high performance. Much of the achievement of highly successful organizations results from the loyal, effective production of down-the-line managers and workers whose power had been unleashed by their leaders, and in the process the followers sensed that their manager/ leaders cared for them in turn.*

Efforts to gain human understanding should dominate a leader's thinking and actions. The leader is neither a statistician nor an engineer, but rather a leader of human beings in a world of Homo sapiens.

What constitutes the manager/leader's job? What is different about the workload of the manager/leader and the nonmanager? What is the nature of the interrelations among peers, subordinates, and superiors?

In attempting to answer such questions some writers have concluded that, contrary to traditional views of organization scholars, manager/leaders do not really plan, organize, implement, and control. Other writers emphasize the great variety in types of activities involved in the work of manager/leaders, the flexibility required, and even the mundane nature of many of the tasks manager/leaders must perform.

To help define what manager/leaders do, let me suggest that they have the following seven major reponsibilities, regardless of their level in the organization. The difference at higher or lower levels in the organization is simply a matter of emphasis. Which of the seven is stressed most will vary from one level to another. For example, a company president clearly would have greater responsibility for and spend more time on coping with strategy than would a department head. However, the department head is not without concern for longer-term strategic matters.

Let us examine the seven important tasks of the manager/leader.

1. *Showing the way.* The substance of any manager/leader's job is grounded in a deep understanding of the organization's basic

41

mission, in other words, on the end result the organization is trying to achieve. Furthermore, the manager/leader must be involved in shaping and articulating the mission to the organization. To be effective, the manager/leader must understand the mission; articulate it clearly, convincingly, and inspiringly; identify the ongoing tasks necessary to achieving the mission; and discipline the organization to always concentrate on those tasks. The understanding of the mission and the ability to express it clearly are often the things that set a person apart as a leader.

2. *Keeping the enterprise viable today.* There is a terrible "nowness" to business. You need a strong today to ensure tomorrow. So the need to get sales is imperative. It drives all the other executive functions—to produce products, solve people problems, meet payrolls, solve technical problems, and the like. The manager/leader must meet and effectively deal with the immediate day-to-day issues. No organization can long survive if today's issues are not dealt with immediately, competently, and vigorously.

3. *Developing and using managing processes.* There is a compelling need to set up a framework within which responsibilities can be delegated on an orderly basis. By operating within such a framework, managers down the line can share in the decision-making in a reasonably orderly way. This permits, even encourages the multiplying power of submanagers—subleaders—in sharing the decision-making and, in the process, adding to their growth. It is imperative that this process both ensures timely decision making and even improves the quality of the decision making. And, of enduring importance, involving subleaders in the decision making process is imperative to their growth and to eventually prepare leaders for greater responsibility.

4. *Coping with the strategic.* The manager/leader needs to be conceptual and imaginative, coupling vision with pragmatism. The leader must balance the short term against the long term

and in the process provide for the future. He/she cannot just tinker with the details of the day-to-day business. Perhaps the organization needs to leap-frog competition. Perhaps it should: move in different directions, or sense external forces and realistically cope with them, or shift to outwit competitive moves. The leader thus crafts a strategy, that is, where the organization is trying to go, and then leads his/her people there.

5. *Developing new leaders.* A prime responsibility of the leader is to ensure continuity of effective managerial leadership by:

   - Identifying those with leadership potential, with such qualities as judgment, energy, motivation, and a basic feel for others.
   - Setting demanding expectations. The tone and drive of any organization is shaped by the expectations imposed on its people. There is a need to create a restless desire to achieve and excel.
   - Providing resources, creative ideas, and motivation. These are the fuels that drive the engine of the organization.
   - Helping subordinates set self-improvement objectives.
   - Following up with coaching on a selective, individual basis.
   - Measuring results and providing feedback, but being careful not to nitpick.
   - Putting managers to work, but not trying to lead everyone personally; rather, leading through sub-leaders.

Successful development of new manager/leaders provides a triple blessing. It enhances the organization, the recipient, and the manager who develops the new manager/leader. The greatest joy and satisfaction, in fact, the highest reward of true leadership that will ever accrue to any leader, is in helping to grow another manager/leader.

6. *Motivating the organization.* The leader must provide the heart and tone of the organization and give it vitality. The manager/leader must generate excitement, "turn the people on," and make the entire experience meaningful. The leader must give his followers hope. Fabius Maximus, the early Roman leader, was noted for his capacity to instill hope in his people. When all of Rome was filled with fear because of the onslaughts of Hannibal, Fabius showed no fear but walked the streets of Rome with an assured and serene countenance. As Plutarch notes, Fabius exhorted the people "not to fear the enemy, but by extraordinary honour to propitiate the gods. This he did not to fill their minds with superstition, but by religious feeling to raise their courage, and lessen their fear of the enemy by inspiring the belief that Heaven was on their side." Fabius succeeded in calming the people and turning their minds to the important task at hand, defending against the Carthaginian terror.

A modern case in point is Robert Crandall, chairman of American Airlines. One of his managers recently told me that when Crandall comes into a group of people, even if you do not know who he is, you can tell by the energy and vibrancy he exudes that he has special capabilities to motivate and spark people. "He is energy in motion," to use the manager's exact words. Crandall's presence has a positive effect on his followers because it inspires optimism, which is to say, it gives them a hopeful sense of the promise of the future.

Plutarch tells us that Alexander the Great had unusual powers of motivation. Apparently when Alexander rode in front of his troops into battle it was like adding two infantry divisions of strength because his soldiers fought with such heightened intensity.

7. *Being the ambassador.* The manager/leader represents his/her people and must be beyond reproach. In his ambassadorship the manager/leader must bring joy and pride to his/her people.

He/she must be a factor in higher headquarters. The leader speaks for the troops. The leader is the symbol of the group, the collective voice for the organization. No group of enthusiastic followers wants to be poorly represented to the organization above and the world around them.

These seven tasks or responsibilities constitute the work of the manager/leader, whether as a president, or a foreman, or a supervisor, or a vice president. The wisdom underlying the skill of leadership is in understanding the emphasis that should be given each of these tasks, according to the particular manager/leader's role in the organization and the situation of the hour. Obviously in a cash-flow crisis the leader must concentrate on No. 2—today's viability. In a case where an organization needs to rebuild its image and outside perception, playing the role of the ambassador becomes most critical and immediate. But over time, the crucial task is to keep a realistic sense of balance in carrying out each of these major tasks and responsibilities.

SETTING DEMANDING EXPECTATION LEVELS

In over forty years of working with organizations on six continents, I found that in all high-performing organizations there were strong demands placed on their managers. It was the Pygmalion effect in which people tended to work up to the level of expectations.

In his important book, *Excellence,* John Gardner summed up one of the most critical challenges facing the industrialized Western world: "We must foster a conception of excellence which may be applied to every degree of ability and to every socially acceptable activity. The tone and fiber of our society depends upon a pervasive and almost universal striving for good performance."

Certainly the level of personal performance expected by the individual executive permeates and affects all other managerial characteristics. The achievement level at which the manager/leader sets his or her sights will have significant impact not only on the manager's own performance, but also on the performance of those under and around him/her. It is true that high expectations are not enough; nor are they any substitute for a total management system, which embraces sound organization structure, effective delegation, meaningful planning, controls, and performance measurement, to mention just a few. However, the converse is equally true. A well-designed organization and management system will sputter and become mushy unless it is driven by expectations of and demands for high performance. And demands for high performance lose their sting unless two things are done:

○ *Giving people resources equal to the level of performance being demanded.* Too often, tough-mindedness is equated with driving people hard rather than with increasing their capacity to produce more through adequate resources, energizing motivation, and sound direction. This represents a subtle but most significant difference. The fact is that demanding high output carries the heavy responsibility of providing resources in the form of ideas, thoughtful direction, adequate authority, or manpower equal to attaining the expected results.

○ *Taking firm action.* Whether it be reward or punishment, there is an important need to give recognition to the quality level of performance and the extent to which the performance meets your expectations. Repeated acceptance of performance that is less than expected will erode the standards of the organization, and it will gradually settle into a lethargic pace at a lower productivity and quality level.

One of the tests of talent in a manager is the extent to which he or she can generate an excitement among followers in their pursuit of demanding goals. And such a power cannot be sustained for long in an organization unless the manager/leader maintains high expectations, continually pursuing excellence both personally and collectively. As James Bryant Conant, a former great from Harvard, expressed it, "Each honest calling, each walk of life, has its own elite, its own aristocracy based on excellence of performance."

To set and achieve demanding levels of expectation takes desire and commitment as well as talent. Speaking of desire and total commitment, I am reminded of the ten-year-old missionary-school boy in India, whose name was Madhu. Little Madhu was extremely fond of his teacher, and as her birthday approached he was most concerned that he had no money to buy her a gift. However, when the day arrived he brought a gift wrapped neatly and carefully in wrinkled brown paper. When the teacher opened the package and beheld its contents, she exclaimed, "How beautiful!" In the package were three perfect, beautifully colored seashells. Then a puzzled look came across the teacher's countenance, and she said, "But Madhu, the ocean is thirty miles away. . . ." She was surprised because she knew that Madhu's family did not have a car. Madhu gazed up at her admiringly and replied, "My long walk is part of your gift."

Commitment to the task and the desire to go the full distance involve the kind of unselfish commitment and desire to please that Madhu demonstrated.

I commented that the expectation level for personal performance permeates all other managerial characteristics. In fact, one can develop an entire philosophy and culture around the concept of Management by Expectation. It would go beyond even Management by Objectives, particularly in an attitudinal sense. This is not to suggest that objectives and goals are not necessary. Indeed they are. But Management by Expectation introduces the concept that much is expected of the individual in the organization. To get maximum results you must do more than merely set goals. You have to instill in people a sense of involvement and then commitment to achieve the goals. There is a need to build a sense of excitement around the goals, a desire on the part of each individual in the organization to want to excel because it means personal development as well as success for the organization. Because doing this suggests a change in attitude, it is difficult to achieve. This is because, at its heart, this approach to leading requires each manager/leader to set the example for his or her followers. While you can inspire and command by words, it is much more important for leaders to inspire by personally showing the way. Getting dedicated, hard work from employees demands a deep and total commitment from the leader. In other words, *demanding much requires giving much.*

Some years ago Frederick R. Kappel (at that time chairman of AT&T) summed this up very well when he said, "Leadership is stating goals that excite people and lift their sights. It is setting the personal example, putting enthusiasm into the operation, communicating both ways (listening as well as talking). It is the right combination of these so that people will do the work that makes a business successful because they want to see it happen."

Probably few other leaders personified the ideal of setting expectation levels by example like President Theodore Roosevelt. His sheer drive and force of character stirred other men to higher levels of performance. His own personal achievement level was so high that no one questioned his right to expect much of others. I remember as a young consultant with McKinsey & Company coming into the office many mornings at 7:30, long before the official start of the business day, to find Marvin Bower, our managing director, already at his desk. His comment to me, which I have never forgotten, was simply, "I not only have to produce much each hour, but I need to do it more hours each day." It was refreshing and revealing as a young man to see the high level of demands he imposed on himself. It was a tremendous motivation to me to get at it early, produce, and work late. I was fortunate to learn this lesson early in my consulting career.

Stanley Crane, the former chairman and CEO who turned around Conrail, expressed it another way. He refers to setting high demands as a "stretching concept." He demands that each person—and he demands it of himself—stretch to reach somewhere beyond where they have been. He is never satisfied with the same level of performance from his people. He always wants more. But what is special, consistent, and characteristic of both Stanley Crane and Marvin Bower is that they are hardest on themselves in the matter of making performance demands. They both realize that to demand much places high and unusual responsibility on the demander. They admit that adherence to this rule was an important factor in their success both as managers and as leaders.

The leader needs vast amounts of physical, spiritual, and psychic energy. Frustrations, disappointments, and "high mountains" will drain energy. The pressure to compete, to make changes, to face the new demands will be physically and emotionally tiring—it will be energy-draining and there is a need to continually replenish the leader's sources of energy.

The effective leader is mentally and emotionally grown up. He/she has matured—is objective and forethoughtful. Such a leader must be free of arrogance and moodiness and realistically well adjusted to life.

Manager/leaders are an organization's most precious asset, therefore, they must manage their own time, talents, and emotions with wisdom and discipline. The old military adage, *As the leader does, so do the troops,* holds true for business organizations. The actions of the leader are always highly visible and carefully watched. In fact, high visibility is both the great privilege and the heavy responsibility of leadership.

There are three aspects of self-management that are crucial to success as a manager/leader. First, high-talent people must concentrate their energies and capacities on high-leverage activities. They must set tough priorities. Such selectivity sets the example for the organization to follow. Second, the manager/leader must be able to sweep aside clutter, cut down on trivia, and make every minute count; in short, he/she must become expert at personal time management. Third, and perhaps the most important element of self-control for manager/leaders is that of managing their own emotions. Leaders are under stress and continuous pressure, which makes it important to their well-being that they maintain an inner calm and peace under fire. Followers desire stability in their leaders and are turned off by a leader who acts like a yo-yo, allowing his or her emotions to soar up and down. Let us examine the three aspects of self-management in greater detail.

Setting Tough Priorities

One of the highest responsibilities of the manager/leader is that of using resources selectively and focusing on areas in which the greatest impact can be made. The leader cannot spend large chunks of time on marginal issues. He/she needs to concentrate personal efforts where it will make the greatest positive difference to the organization. It is no doubt true that something like 20 percent of any manager/leader's efforts will produce 80 percent of his results. One of the tragedies of our industrial experience is the percentage of time capable manager/leaders and other key people down the line are heavily involved in carrying out relatively unimportant or marginal activities. Setting and living priorities is not so much an intellectual process as it is a matter of discipline and mental toughness. It is easy to follow the philosophy of giving a little bit for everything for two reasons. First, we are often afraid not to spread our resources over every possible activity for fear we might miss something. Second, we fail to discipline ourselves to make the mental effort of sorting out the important from the unimportant. Using resources selectively requires the manager to decide what products, what markets, what distribution channels, and what "end product uses" should be the focus of the efforts and resources of his or her people. This task of making choices and setting priorities is among the toughest that humans must cope with. The secret to setting tough priorities is to nurture one's *instinct for the essential.* The pivotal job of the manager/leader is deploying effectively the assets under his control, particularly his own time and talent.

How activities are carried out is important but making certain that key people are working on the right things is of equal consequence. The easiest and safest policy is to spread any organization's resources over the widest number of opportunities with the hope, of course, that nothing is missed. *Managerial progress will come, however, only when manager/leaders courageously assign the organization's and their own primary resources to high-leverage opportunities while eliminating marginal activities.* In summary, there is too much preoccupation by manager/leaders with how to do things right. This reflects their desire for efficiency. What is needed is more attention to first determining what are the right things to do. There is nothing more futile than developing grand solutions to mundane opportunities, or doing the irrelevant well.

There is a pervasive need for the manager/leader to be selective, that is, to determine where to concentrate energies and talents. *Nowhere is the judicious allocation of resources more important than in the way the manager/leader uses his or her personal time.* The manager/leader cannot allocate major resources or important tasks in his or her organization if he or she is bogged down in unimportant or irrelevant minutia. Despite this, the days of most manager/leaders are filled with relatively unimportant tasks—many of which are thrust upon them. There is today an increased premium on selectivity because of the high cost of assets and tools of production (labor, energy, machines). Also, pressure on margins and increased competition reduces tolerance for wasting resources on less than the highest quality opportunities. We must learn how to use less better.

If one is to survive and grow as a manager/leader, it is imperative that one identify the relatively few things that will make the greatest difference and then concentrate on them. The hardest thing to do, particularly from the standpoint of the aggressive manager/leader, is to avoid working on every problem or opportunity that presents itself. Focusing sharply on this would require the manager/leader to identify all of the important areas in which he or she can make a significant impact. This may include the key people with whom the manager/leader should spend the most time, the kind of planning activities to engage in, and where to concentrate decision-making attention. As the key asset within his or her sphere of organization, the manager/leader must allocate personal priorities as judiciously as those of the rest of the organization. In summary, to set tough priorities, the manager/leader must:

○ Think in terms of end results. Emphasize accomplishment, not activity.
○ Avoid taking involved positions on everything.
○ Discard the trivial; avoid trying to do the irrelevant superbly.
○ Concentrate on doing the right things, not just on doing them well.
○ Think in terms of cost versus benefits in setting personal priorities.
○ Finally, work diligently to release the power of others.

Managing Time

The most pervasive and burdensome problem of manager/leaders is to find enough time. That has been a problem for high-performing leaders since the beginning of recorded history. It boils down to the simple fact that the manager/leader continually faces the nitty-gritty struggle of how to get more done each hour and each day.

The basic prerequisite to improving one's management of time is developing the right frame of mind. There is likely to be a high correlation between one's degree of desire and good use of time. It takes push, drive, and sustained effort to constantly discipline oneself to produce. It calls for nurturing a sense of urgency, to constantly keep in mind the desire to get the next job done, and do it quickly.

One perennial barrier to achieving the right frame of mind is the belief often held that in order to think effectively one must be in exactly the right location and under the right circumstances. In many cases, postponing meditative effort or hard thinking may simply be a stalling tactic—an unwillingness to take on the tough task of thinking.

The real crux of time management is how to make use of small pieces of time that become available throughout the day. The manager/leader's life is a disrupted one, so the real skill is not concentration alone but the ability to immediately turn your total concentrative powers to the single task at hand and, when this is done, to move without delay to the next task. This means developing the discipline and art of effectively using small pieces of time that fall between the normal periods of daily disruptions.

Let me give you a few facts—or perhaps they should be labeled "researched opinions"—that may drive home more effectively the value of time management.

- Surveys indicate that executives themselves believe they are wasting two to four hours each day on unnecessary trivia. That is a significant percentage of the average executive's working day.
- An AMA survey some years ago found that the typical executive spends as much as three hours each day reading letters, memoranda, business articles, reports, and the like. That is equal to more than 25 percent of his/her working day. Tests also show that the usual executive's reading speed is 250 words per minute, and that with disciplined practice this speed can be increased without too much difficulty to over 400 words per minute, obviously an effective way to find more time.
- Other studies show that the well-educated person sustains himself at a deep level of concentration for only two to three minutes at a time. A significant amount of the creative output of executives is the result of a few such two- or three-minute periods sprinkled throughout the day. Studies also show that through forceful self-discipline and dedicated practice, these brief periods of intense effectiveness can be expanded from 50 to 100 percent—to four and one-half to six minutes—and that they can be experienced more frequently.

I leave you with two thoughts on the subject: Continually force yourself to concentrate on the high-priority tasks and brush aside the clutter; and drive your mind consistently throughout the day to concentrate solely on the one task at hand and get it done, then turn immediately to the next. The real crux of the problem is how much you can get done in the next five minutes.

Managing One's Emotions

The manager/leader's life is hectic, and he or she operates under pressure; therefore, patience can wear thin quickly and counter-productive emotions explode. The mature leader needs a high boiling point—a high flash point. "Big" leaders rarely "blow up." Instead, they reserve displays of anger for critical situations when they will be effective in turning the tide in a negotiating situation or in motivating people, such as a board of directors, to do the right thing in reaching a major decision.

Adding to the frustration of the manager/leader's life is the need to cope with uncertainty and ambiguity. For example, relationships with superiors and subordinates can never be completely described in advance, so the manager/leader must continually feel his or her way by probing and testing and, to some extent, developing tactics as situations unfold. All of which means that the manager/leader is constantly dealing with relationships that have a degree of uncertainty and ambiguity.

Alexander the Great (in the fourth century B.C.) was an extreme case of a leader who had towering strengths but was severely handicapped by violent swings in emotion. He frequently went into blind rages and on more than one occasion he killed a good companion with his sword. Such outbursts would be followed by long periods of deep depression and remorse. In addition, Alexander was apparently addicted to alcohol, which complicated his emotional instability and perhaps contributed to health problems culminating in death at only thirty-two years of age. It has always taxed my imagination to ponder what additional heroic and great deeds Alexander might have accomplished had he lived a few more years or avoided so many useless days when he was incapacitated by depression. His inability to manage his emotions was indeed a heavy cross to bear.

Each manager/leader must wrestle with and gain control over his or her own inner anxieties and emotions while radiating a high degree of self-confidence. There are two important things to think about here; one is that few people respond well to a leader who has erratic swings in emotions or who more than infrequently loses self-control and blows up. This makes it imperative that one's own emotions be held within reasonable constraints.

Perhaps even more important is developing what can be called an inner calm, an imperturbable manner that permits the manager/leader to face the unexpected, the disappointments and pressures of leadership, without experiencing self-destructive anger, frustration, and impatience. The leader needs to develop a serenity of the soul. Clearly one of President Ronald Reagan's great strengths was his internal serenity—an ability to make difficult decisions without fretting and excessive worrying. Without such an inner calm or peace, it would be difficult, if not impossible, to keep pace and sustain quality thinking at the level of energy necessary to a highly productive manager/leader in our industrial or institutional society.

Not only must the manager/leader possess an attitude that refuses to "get down," he or she needs to continually lift the spirits of others. This calls for spreading the gospel of positive thinking, radiating the strength of genuine enthusiasm. Only as the leader improves the psyche of others will his or her own mental outlook be improved. The manager/leader cannot do this with personal emotions that are not under control. Perhaps a good case in point is Barry Sullivan, former chairman of the First Chicago Corporation (First National Bank). It is quite apparent that Mr. Sullivan had his problems (particularly large, bad loans), frustrations, and disappointments during his first several years at the bank. He walked into a tough situation that continued to be demanding of his energy and patience. He did a remarkable job in keeping his cool and managing his emotions in a controlled, mature way. Some have labeled him "unflappable." While there are many other factors involved in his leadership, the fact that he has maintained his "cool" gives him an aura of maturity and sets a fine example for the other officers and managers in the bank.

The effective manager/leader must have a capacity for abstraction, vision and the ability to conceptualize. The leader must have great facility to translate the conceptual into concrete specifics that are readily understood and meaningful to the people in the organization. This is translating vision into reality.

Christopher Galvin, president of Motorola, recently said that "the art of management starts with vision." I agree, because to me the sine qua non of effective leadership is the ability to instill throughout the organization a sense of purpose. This means that the substance of any manager/leader's job must be grounded in a deep understanding of the organization's basic mission. It is the end product of what the organization is trying to achieve. It cannot be a mere statement of a vague goal no matter how lofty its aim or how stirring its language. The "mission" must be a clearly defined purpose toward which the leader is taking the organization. The leader's vision embraces all of the factors critical to achieving the mission, and his or her daily tasks add up to relentless step-by-step and day-to-day attention to doing those things that move the organization toward its goal. Galvin further has called leadership "the catalyst needed to transform talent into results." Sometimes indeed the work of an effective manager/leader can appear to exhibit precisely the kind of biochemical reaction implied by the word *catalyst*. But the role of the leader is more logical and can be summarized as follows: *The effective manager/leader must understand the mission, even help shape it, articulate it convincingly and inspiringly, identify the ongoing tasks important to achieving the mission, and discipline the organization to always concentrate on those tasks that contribute to progress toward the mission.*

Leadership by definition is goal-oriented. Manager/leaders lead people toward something, defining the mission and persuading their followers that the goal is worth achieving. In doing so, they create cohesion among a random collection of individuals. The leaders direct the attention of followers toward a common purpose, inspiring each one of them to work for the mutual good. The goal may be as commonplace as beating a competitor in a football game or as vital as winning a war. The dynamics of leadership are the same. There must be a goal, it must be clearly defined, and the people must perceive—be persuaded—that its attainment is worthwhile to the organization and, in some sense, to them. Achieving the mission requires leaders to inspire their people to think in terms of results, emphasizing accomplishment rather than activity and avoiding preoccupation with technique. In everything they say and do, manager/leaders communicate that the purpose of the organization is to achieve a predetermined goal. It is not merely to create processes, follow procedures, or perfect methods. Every decision manager/leaders make, every task they assign, must help to point their people toward accomplishing those things vital to success. Every expenditure of resources must be weighed in terms of its probable contribution to the accomplishment of the organization's mission.

Pope John Paul II is credited with many accomplishments during his papacy, but his most important achievement, Catholic scholars agree, was in restoring a clear sense of what the church stands for. Concentrating on achieving the mission requires manager/leaders to identify the few important goals to achieve; inspire their people to think in terms of end results; emphasize accomplishment, not activity; and avoid preoccupation with technique. In brief, manager/leaders must thoroughly understand those factors critical to success in their business. Some express this as identifying the areas of leverage, others refer to it as determining how money is made. In the case of church leaders, it is how souls are won.

I am always reminded of IBM when I think of dedication to mission. One of the hallmarks of IBM's success has been an unswerving dedication to fulfilling the product (hardware and software applications) and service needs of their customers so superbly that customers have virtually no choice when deciding from whom to buy their next computer. The beauty of IBM's mission is its simplicity: to always, in everything they do, be customer-focused, customer-driven. And it is compelling to note that the heart of the problem and struggles IBM has today probably results from a diminution in its former dedication to that mission.

General Clarence Lindsey, in a speech at Northwestern University, said that the mission of the Air Force was to "fly and fight and help keep the peace." A bishop of the Roman Catholic Church at the Vatican once told me that the basic mission of the Church is to "save souls." These simple statements of mission become particularly powerful when manager/leaders emphasize the message by ensuring that their every action and communication furthers their organization's capacity to achieve these few things. Such singleness of purpose at the top enhances the ability of subleaders all the way down the chain of command to relate their day-to-day activities to achieving the mission.

Leaders emerge quickly in a crisis or under challenging conditions because at such times the person who can define and reinforce the goals can lead the group. When manager/leaders fail to define the goals during normal times the result is a lack of esprit de corps in the organization and a feeling of drifting. Conversely, nothing is more exhilarating or motivational than an organization whose people have a strong sense of their mission. The sense of purpose, of knowing where they are going, instills spirit and drive in employees. It provides a good deal of the spark necessary to accomplishment.

St. Paul gave us a powerful message about a sense of mission when he wrote to his followers in Philippi, "I press toward the mark." The message sets forth a clear sense of direction and an urgency to reach the objective—his followers knew clearly what Paul meant by "the mark" and they also felt the urgency and "heat" of this desire to move forward, to push relentlessly toward the target.

Stamina is the leader's ultimate resource. Little is much good without endurance. This is evidenced by the ability to work long and hard, especially under pressure or after disappointment. I recall a corporate president recently saying, "My greatest strength grows out of my tenacity." Life and leadership both are more of a marathon than a dash.

The leader needs the capacity to meet adversity without succumbing to emotional paralysis or withdrawal and without lashing out at colleagues or subordinates. One significant test of quality leadership is how well the leader copes with disappointments, defeat, or some form of overriding adversity. Voltaire, in praising this quality in the Duke of Marlborough, called it "calm courage in the midst of tumult, that serenity of soul in danger, which is the greatest gift of nature for command."

During the past two decades scholars in behavioral studies have tended to diminish the importance of leadership traits as primary indicators of leadership capacity. It is generally agreed that the mere possession of so-called important or acceptable traits is not a guarantee of success as a leader. I accept that conclusion. However, identifying and examining leadership traits is not an unproductive exercise. The aspiring leader can learn much from others who have already demonstrated leadership skills and accomplishments. One thing that distinguishes the Homo sapien from the other animals is his or her ability to learn from the experience of others, and each new generation has the potential, not always realized, of starting on the shoulders of its predecessors. We learn how to lead from those who have preceded us because basic traits of leadership do not change, even though leadership styles and the application of techniques indeed may and do change. Certainly the marvelous concept so forcefully expressed by Plato over 2,300 years ago—that *we should govern for the benefit of the governed*—has remained immutable. By the same token, we can gain from the leadership experience of others. The real value of identifying and evaluating leadership traits is in the extent to which we can use them to draw lessons from the experiences and lives of others. This does not suggest that we will necessarily try to develop the same traits another possesses or assume that by learning a certain trait we can become a successful manager/leader. However, understanding what seems to work or not work for others can be applied in shaping our individual approach to leadership.

With that in mind, it should be helpful to turn to the experiences of current business leaders. David Goode, CEO of one of the nation's largest and most profitable transportation companies, the Norfolk Southern Corporation. David Goode says he believes that six leadership characteristics have been most critical in his own career.

1. *Generating loyalty in his followers.* To do this Goode feels he must be among the troops—he must be seen. He is a great believer in the "management by walking around" theory. As a result, his people believe that their CEO understands them and their aspirations.
2. *Making a total commitment to the company.* The company is his life and his troops know it. They know he places the company and its people before his/her own interests.
3. *Being, and being perceived to be, completely fair.* There is a feeling among Goode's executives and managers that the chief will always deal off the "top of the deck," that he will never take advantage of them.
4. *Demonstrating great trust in his/her managers.* Goode believes this is a necessary prerequisite to having managers in turn trust him. Trust begets trust. No one is allowed to play games. Goode insists on openness and candor in dealing with one another. There is no tolerance for being coy or cozy.

5. *Developing an in-depth understanding of the business and the capacity to use that knowledge and experience in making the right choices.* Goode feels he must demonstrate that he is a real business professional and that his people must believe that he truly understands the business.

6. *Emphasizing that it is important never to be a "phony."* Goode believes that the good leader is always what he claims to be. His people know who and what he is and what he stands for because he consistently tries to live what he believes.

In discussing these traits, Goode emphasized that it is not enough to merely live them; people in the organization must also perceive them to be so. The perception of what the leader believes in and is becomes just as important as the fact of what he is.

Let's look at another business leader, Thomas Donohue, president and CEO of the United States Chamber of Commerce and formerly the president and CEO of The American Trucking Associations. Mr. Donohue exemplifies several traits or personal characteristics that I believe have been vital to his continuing success.

1. *He listens.* Donohue is patient and works at convincing his troops that he has heard them. The result is an empathy between him and his people.

2. *He demonstrates consistency in attitude and performance.* Donohue's actions and reactions are reasonably predictable because he does not "lose his cool." He avoids acting like an "emotional yo-yo" in his reactions and relations to people and events.

3. *He concentrates on thinking problems through without getting tangled in the "underbrush of complexity."* Donohue feels that he has a "gift" for doing this, for being able to simplify what others regard as complex issues.

4. *He shares ideas.* Asking his managers for input on his own cre-

ative thoughts makes them feel the ideas are really theirs or at least partly theirs. As a result, Donohue he gets great support and commitment for bringing about the changes he wants.

5. *Finally, and most importantly, Tom Donohue believes it is imperative to be absolutely open.* This builds total trust—as it goes both ways. He believes strongly that unless there is trust, people will not willingly follow a leader.

Over the past ten years, I have surveyed over one thousand executives on what they thought were the ten most important traits of an effective manager/leader. While these answers ranged over a wide number of traits, there seemed to be a reasonable consensus on the following composite list of the most important traits.

1. Capacity to motivate or inspire, to generate excitement, to turn people on, to be alive.
2. A sense of confidence and enthusiasm.
3. Sensitivity to others; empathy; "feeding" the troops; caring for their followers.
4. Intelligence and knowledge; the perception of competence. Truly knowing your business and using this expertise in a professional way.
5. Being present at key moments; being available when the troops need you. *This is the rationale behind the concept of "walking around" management but it goes further. It is not so important how often you walk around but that you have made it your business to be there when the going is rough for your people.*
6. Avoiding the appearance of arrogance. People do not willingly follow arrogance and invariably resent it.
7. Never being timid or tentative. Followers respect decisiveness in a business leader and unhesitating courage in the military officer (even though he may be filled with fear). Lead from up front.
8. Never being petty or small, never destroying a person's digni-

ty, never being mean or seeking retribution out of spite. While Lee Iaccoca is a splendid business leader who was wronged by Henry Ford, the way he permitted his hatred of Mr. Ford to fester (according to the press) is a part of Iaccoca that I would like to forget—a part that I wish *he* would forget.

9. Being and being perceived to be open, being above board; no "game playing." *It is imperative to be what you present yourself to be.*

10. Being effective in deciding without being either rash or tentative; making decisions confidently, without arrogance.

Power of Accessibility

William Smithburg, former chairman and chief executive officer of the Quaker Oats Company, is a great believer that you must enjoy everything you do, work as well as play. In addition, a great part of his managerial strength stems from his knowledge of his organization, of what his people are doing and what they need to succeed. Smithburg sees his people frequently and is seen by them. He is accessible, which is an important ingredient in problem solving and decision making. Being accessible is also vital in assuring down-the-line managers that the leader is caring and committed.

Capacity to Make Decisions

Mastering the art (and it is more art than science) of making decisions is critical to effective managerial leadership. Vernon Loucks, chairman of Baxter International, says that he is "comfortable in making decisions, big or small." He believes that his sense of "comfort" comes through to his followers and that a sense of comfort on the part of the leader conveys a feeling of confidence that impacts positively on the organization. A good sense of timing is essential for effective decision making. One must know when to end the discussions, deliberations, and attempts to generate consensus and make the decision. A true sense of comfort and confidence in the decision-making process is based on the manager/leader's willingness to face up to whatever the consequence might be for a particular decision. Vernon Loucks feels this is much more than bravado: it is being downright realistic and practical. Obviously excessive fear and worry about consequences is an impediment and often delays or even postpones the decision-making process. Such "hesitation" by the manager/leader fosters a feeling in the organization that its leadership is tentative, unsure of itself, or even wishy-washy. But the opposite problem can and does exist—an excessively impulsive or hip-shooting type of decision making. There is no simple set of criteria to determine how quickly to act. Some issues require instant response and fast decision making. Other problems or opportunities require a more calculated approach. Therein lies the managerial leader judgment—the art of determining the type of approach and timing that is appropriate for making the individual decision.

The Power of Stamina

I know of no effective leader who does not have stamina and exhibit great energy. Being a successful manager/leader requires great energy—physical, emotional, and spiritual. If the leader is to motivate his/her followers, he/she must exude confidence, enthusiasm (from a Greek word meaning "inspired by some divinity"), and persuasiveness. Indeed it is difficult for an unenthusiastic or lackadaisical person to be very persuasive. Followers by definition look for qualities of strength and evidence of confidence, both of which are reinforced by stamina and endurance. The leader's ultimate resources are stamina, tenacity, and perseverance. Nothing is much good without endurance. The ability to work consistently hard and long especially under pressure is the mark of a strong, surviving leader.

Manifesting these qualities on a continuing basis, under the stresses that occur in the manager/leader's life, requires deep reserves of physical and emotional strength. I know of no effective, mature manager/leader who does not have and expend unusual amounts of energy and endurance. It takes energy, stamina, and endurance to be an effective and highly productive person. Even Gandhi, the strong, wise leader of India—a wisp of a man—had great aliveness and enormous staying power. His aliveness inspired a whole subcontinent of followers. To be successful in what you are doing requires great energy—physical, emotional, and spiritual. Talent and intelligence are not enough. Without endurance these do not go far enough.

Ecclesiastes notes that the race does not necessarily go to the swift. The challenge is to keep running. So it is true in business. What often counts the most is the capacity to work consistently long and hard, especially under pressure and after disappointing setbacks. A battered mind and abused body are true handicaps in our fast-track, super mobile business world. Our hospitals and cemeteries give mute testimony to those unable to handle modern-day stresses and temptations.

To keep coming back day after day requires the discipline of pacing oneself—it takes endurance. I have seen strong leaders who unfortunately too frequently have to withdraw because they cannot consistently stand the heat. Having endurance in business means the capacity to take the "heat," to keep coming back each day fresh for another round. Many lack the stamina to stay in the race. Thus not only does maintaining a high energy level foster getting a lot done, it also energizes other people within the organization.

Perhaps the finest example of these characteristics has been demonstrated by Pope John Paul II. Few leaders have ever exhibited his stamina in visiting and serving his followers—even traveling to the ends of the earth. The Pope's schedule would wear out men half his age. He has great staying power. He seems to have the courage and capacity to move into difficult situations and stay with them until they are resolved. His 1985 trip to the liberal-minded Dutch church was a real test in grit and inner toughness coupled with a magnificent desire to bring the "wanderers" back into the fold.

It is very apparent that effective leaders, to put it bluntly, work hard. Some years ·ago, I had dinner with a successful German businessman in Frankfort. I asked him his formula for achieving success. He said there were but three requirements: "Werk, Werk, und Werk."

Leo F. Mullin, president and CEO of Delta Airlines, states that he is a high-energy person. He is a man who can handle an extremely heavy work schedule with a minimum of fatigue and the capacity to bounce right back after periods of intensive work. Clearly it is difficult to become an effective leader and a high achiever without the capacity to consistently endure a heavy work schedule and actually get a sense of joy out of it.

The leader's ultimate resource is stamina, tenacity, and perseverance and the basis for all three is superb health, energy, and drive. Nothing is much good without endurance. The critical talent of the leader is the ability to work consistently hard and long, particularly under pressure, disappointment, or even pain. Pain is not synonymous with or necessary to success, but truly overcoming obstacles develops character and is the mark of true class. The Apostle Paul achieved greatness and is remembered through history as one who constantly had to overcome the "thorn in his flesh." Clearly he was driven by a spiritual fire and his capacity to endure hardship and overcome obstacles set him apart from ordinary men and, indeed, was at the core of his splendid leadership of men.

I remember the words of a military historian on this subject. The gist of his comments was that the first battle is won by speed, readiness, and powerful forces. But the subsequent battles and the war are won largely by endurance and sustainability—the capacity to continue to slug it out longer than the enemy and to simply wear them out—to come out new and refreshed each morning for a new day of battle.

Capacity to Synthesize

The manager/leader must have the capacity to synthesize, which means the ability to take scraps of information or masses of data and shape it into usable knowledge. Napoleon was a military leader who had a special ability to synthesize. He could take scraps of information from reconnaissance parties and piece them together to form a remarkably comprehensive battle plan. It was his capacity to visualize the whole from scattered bits of information that made him such a brilliant military tactician. So it is in any other type of organization. The leader works with inadequate information out of which he must fashion a mission and a plan of action, a definition of where he wants to take the organization.

Drive to Excel

No one can succeed as a manager/leader without the drive to excel. This requires deep inner reserves of energy. The Apostle Paul, as recorded in the New Testament, achieved greatness and is remembered through history as one who constantly had to endure hardship and overcome major obstacles. Clearly he was driven by an inner spiritual energy that gave him the strength to lead—and to teach courage and commitment by his own example. This was one of the principal characteristics that set Paul apart from ordinary men. Certainly it is difficult to become a high achiever without the capacity to consistently carry a heavy work schedule—especially under pressure and after disappointing setbacks. Followers, by definition, look for qualities of strength and self-confidence and a positive attitude in their leaders. To motivate and persuade people requires considerable enthusiasm. To manifest these qualities requires a deep inner reserve of energy and the willingness to always draw on that reserve selflessly.

Power of Presence

Above all else, the manager/leader must be present among his people. As Walt Whitman, the great American poet, said, "I and mine do not convince by arguments; we convince by our presence."

Let me cite two examples that strongly illustrate the power of presence. A few years ago, you will remember, a United Airlines crew brought down a crippled DC-10 jet airliner in the cornfields of Iowa, miraculously saving the lives of many of the passengers. Stephen Wolfe, then chairman of United, was at the scene of the crash within a few hours. He spoke to the families of those who lost their lives with the simple but effective words, "I am Stephen Wolfe, Chairman of

United. This is my airplane. I am deeply sorry this happened. While we cannot bring any of the victims back to life, we will do everything in our power to be helpful."

Contrast this with what happened at Valdez, Alaska, in 1990 when the Exxon tanker went aground and spilled several million barrels of oil in the waters off the Alaska coast. Lawrence Rawls, chairman of Exxon, never personally went to the scene of the accident. While I do not know his inner feelings, I would suspect that he has regretted his decision to stay away. The media accounts suggested that the chairman was following the advice of his legal and public relations departments to stay away. At the time, I was in Washington, D.C., attending meetings with oil industry executives. They all expressed the hope that Lawrence Rawls would go to Alaska and publicly apologize.

Never Be Petty or Small

The manager/leader also must be above pettiness. He or she must not think or act small, or as de Gaulle put it, "Be not like ordinary men who splash in shallow water." Choose the high road and your followers will be uplifted.

Power of Integrity and Courage

Integrity and courage are the qualities that truly distinguish a leader. As I emphasize elsewhere in this book: integrity (which begets trust) is the foundation stone of voluntary followership and leadership. Courage in war is defined as bravery in the face of danger. In our normal day-to-day life, courage is the unwavering strength to do what we believe is right in the face of tough opposition, to do the hard tasks with grace and without hesitation. Courage is never tentative nor is the leader unwilling to take the hard position. It is imperative to recognize that it is impossible to achieve effective voluntary leadership in the absence of integrity and courage. Lack of integrity destroyed the leadership capabilities of religious evangelists Jimmy Bakker and Jimmy Swaggert, especially since they held themselves up as paragons of virtue.

The 1988 and 1992 Republican and Democratic presidential campaigns threw an interesting light on the issue of leadership. In these campaigns the issue of leadership ability became a real concern for the American people. No wonder, for they were subjected to much disillusionment. Perhaps most significant was the numbing realization that the once-towering leadership of Ronald Reagan seemed to be fading. The high-flying Gary Hart, almost certain to be a nominee, was suddenly dumped from contention because of questions regarding his morality and judgment. Joseph Biden, an eloquent, bright, and charismatic senator who possessed many leadership qualities, suddenly had to withdraw because public perceptions cast doubt on his integrity. And the 1996 presidential campaign was no exception. The issue of character and integrity was at the heart of that campaign also.

Leadership Characteristics in Summary

What is there about leadership that causes so many aspirants to stumble? This is a complex question to which there are no quick answers. But here are some thoughts on it. Our perception of leaders turns on small but important actions. Remember my previous example of the manly demonstration by the wounded President Reagan. His capacity to remain calm and serene in moments of crisis and stress were reactions that followers particularly admire in their leaders. Perhaps what it boils down to is simply that voters—or followers—search for evidence of strength of character. Clearly character was at the very heart of the 1988 presidential campaign, as it was in the 1992, and 1996, and likely in any future campaign. The candidates in different ways played a common theme—that they had the type of character that could be trusted. Several articles prior to the Republican convention suggested that compassion was the major theme of candidates George Bush, Bob Dole, and Jack Kemp. They extolled such virtues as "sensitivity," "helping people," and "ensuring rights." They all wanted to be thought of as "servant leaders," to show that they had concern for the people. And beneath all this was a pervasive desire to convince the public that they could be trusted. This is not to suggest that strength of character or the perception of trust and integrity are all that is needed to win a presidential campaign. The germ truth is simply that without integrity and trust, nothing else matters. Trust is the bedrock on which all democratic leadership is founded. So in the process of building a political candidate—even in the shaping of a party's platform—great stress is placed on "the trust factor." However many requirements one names as essential for effective leadership, they all begin and end with quality of character, anchored in integrity and trust.

There is nothing magic about leadership; it comes about because the leader's presence, in a sense, expresses the sum total of his/her life, goals, ideals, and values; and these traits, in turn, are perceived and appreciated by his/her followers.

The capacity to articulate is the sine qua non of effective leadership. As Disraeli so incisively expressed it, "Men command by words." But effective articulation requires both understanding as well as being understood.

Leadership requires good communications between the manager/ leader and his or her people. The followers must understand the leader's objectives, policies and instructions, and the leader must learn from them what is happening throughout the organization and be alert to their needs as well as to their ideas for advancing the enterprise.

- The manager/leader must be able to express ideas, values, and expectations in order to convey a sense of the organization's mission to subordinates. Articulation—the ability to write and speak—is vital to effective leadership.
- At the same time, the manager/leader must encourage the flow of accurate information upward from the followers. If that doesn't happen, his or her decisions will be ill-founded and difficult to implement.
- In that vein also, the manager/leader must foster the exchange of information among subordinates and between his or her unit and other departments so that cooperation and cross-pollination of ideas is encouraged and facilitated.

Despite the importance of being able to exchange information accurately by speaking, writing, and listening, manager/leaders often fail to work on developing these skills in themselves and in their subordinates.

As the demands on manager/leaders grow, so does their need to articulate effectively. Managerial leaders—whether foremen, supervisors, vice presidents, or CEOs—daily find themselves expressing ideas and persuading people into action. Clearly, the effective leader does much of this by example; but there is no substitute for the ability to accurately and forcefully communicate ideas orally and in writing. The use of words, which is the expression of our ideas and thoughts, is so commonplace that we tend to forget its power. As Disraeli said, "Men command by words."

History is replete with examples of how facility with words was critical to leadership success.

> ○ Moses, when called by the Lord to lead the Israelite people from Egyptian bondage, lamented his inability to speak with authority. As recorded in Exodus, he replied, "Oh, my Lord, I am not eloquent, I am slow of tongue." As we know from the story, Moses spoke through the mouth of Aaron his brother. So Moses knew the value of eloquence in speaking.
> ○ Alexander the Great led his armies to march through and conquer much of the known world in the third century B.C. Plutarch in his *Lives* tells us of Alexander's mastery in exhorting his men to undergo unbelievable hardship and overcome overwhelming odds in their heroic march to India.
> ○ Or remember Marcellus, the great Roman proconsul and leader of the Roman armies in their long struggle against Hannibal from Carthage. At his trial before the Roman Senate for alleged atrocities at Syracuse, Marcellus in dramatic voice not only won over the Roman leaders but also his accusers from Syracuse.
> ○ Or Brutus, who with unmatched eloquence (as told to us by Shakespeare) won over the angry Roman populace after the assassination of Julius Caesar.
> ○ Or in more recent times, Winston Churchill when he steeled the allied nations with his flaming eloquence. I remember hearing a transmission by radio of his forever famous, "We will fight

on the beaches, we will fight in the streets, we will never give up." Clearly his words helped galvanize a whole nation and much of the world in that hour of peril.

- Or President Franklin Roosevelt, following the attack on Pearl Harbor, when he gave his stirring "a date which will live in infamy" speech that moved Congress to declare war.
- Or the legendary Knute Rockne, who spurred on his famous Notre Dame football team by inspiring them to "win one for the Gipper," a popular deceased player whom he felt was somewhere up in the sky looking down on Notre Dame's fortunes.
- Or John F. Kennedy, when he charged the nation with his "ask not what your country can do for you, but what you can do for your country."
- And finally, skilled television articulation did much to make of Ronald Reagan a governor and then a president.

There is overwhelming evidence of a close correlation between leadership and the capacity to express ideas, particularly in speech. Language facility is a sine qua non of effective leadership.

However, there is another side to the need for speaking clearly and that is—*listening intently and with understanding.* Expressed in a different way, it is necessary to first understand, that you might in turn be better understood.

The good communications required between the manager/leader and his or her people is a two-way system. The followers must indeed understand the leader, but it is equally important that the leader first listen to them. It is a sending and receiving process. The receiving is often more difficult—it takes energy and concentration to listen with understanding. You cannot send well, however, if you are not getting clear reception. I am reminded of the beautiful thought from the prayer of St. Francis, "Lord, grant that I may not seek so much to be understood as to understand."

Listening is an art too seldom practiced. Without good listeners, there are no effective speakers. Good listening requires the expenditure of energy in paying attention. It requires total concentration on what is being said, driving all other thoughts from your mind, particularly those about what you plan to say next. Listening is an active, mental process, and it must be leavened with a lot of patience if there is to be understanding. After all, the purpose of both speaking and listening is to gain understanding, to instruct or to learn as a basis for taking constructive action. A corporate president who commented on the need for two-way communication in an organization said he is guided by the concept that "leadership is communication in action." You cannot speak meaningfully in a leadership situation unless first you have listened and understood your audience.

Perhaps out of the foregoing paragraph we could summarize a few simple rules for listening well.

1. *Be, and appear to be, receptive.* The most important part of listening is to convince the speaker that you are truly listening. After all, that is the main objective of the speaker, that you hear and understand.
2. *Be physically active and alert.* Avoid having a faraway look in your eyes. Be intent and give the speaker 100 percent of your mental and physical attention.
3. *Try hard to understand.* Be serious about understanding. Interrupt the speaker only if you need clarity to understand a point.
4. *Replay your understanding.* When the speaker has finished, replay your understanding of what was said. In this way you assure him or her that you have understood even if you do not agree.
5. *Know your people.* You must go beyond just hearing the words spoken. You must understand why your people take a certain position or express a point of view. What is happening that is shaping their point of view?

Richard Ferris, formerly chairman of United Airlines, emphasizes that listening to people is his first rule of good management. This precept takes on added significance in view of Mr. Ferris's very positive and strong-willed style of management. Christopher Galvin, president of Motorola, replied when asked about the important ingredients of his business success that he could sum it up quickly: "I listen and learn." Galvin points out that his reasons for listening are several, but most importantly he listens intently to give his people a genuine sense of participation and involvement in the management process. He also said that listening is the key to gaining acceptance of his plans and a willingness on the part of his people to implement the decisions coming out of his office. Finally Galvin has found that effective listening is often a good source of ideas. He believes that his decisions are better because he has listened.

Richard Morrow, the former chief executive of the Amoco Corporation, singles out as one of his leadership strengths the "capacity and patience to listen." Morrow carefully sought out the views of his people in the process of making decisions. And he made some bold decisions in the few years after he inherited the job from John Swearingen—decisions such as expanding overseas and engineering a $1.7 billion stock repurchase plan. Morrow's ability to listen well has undoubtedly helped him gain a keen sense of what his organization is capable of implementing and has instilled greater confidence in his decision-making process.

This is not to say that eloquence or clarity of expression is enough. It obviously requires more than that to lead. The importance of speaking clearly—and yes, even with feeling or eloquence—is the extent to which it helps drive home a message to the listeners. Facility with words can increase the perception of leadership. Followers are moved by words that have a ring of substance, sincerity, and compassion. But above all else the message must be clearly understood by the followers, both intellectually and emotionally.

The leader must be an extraordinary agent for change and discontinuities.
The leader must be out front to encourage change and growth and to show
the way to bring it about. There are two important requisites to bringing
about change:

- *Knowing the technical requirements.*
- *Understanding the attitudinal and motivation*
  demands for bringing it about.

Vital is the need to convert an organization unaccustomed to change
to one that can not only accept but can manage rapidly occurring
changes. My purpose here is not to present a lengthy treatise on the
whole change process; that is a book in itself. But rather I want to
emphasize that one of the major challenges faced by manager/leaders
is to be able to identify and effectively bring about meaningful
change. As Charles F. "Boss" Kettering of General Motors said some
years ago, "Change is the only thing that has ever brought progress."
It is interesting to observe the great variations in the capacity of business organizations to both identify the need and to bring about
change. Some have had remarkable success—others have sputtered
and floundered. Here are a few of the important steps taken by successful companies to bring about the kind of change that is demanded in today's difficult business climate.

- *Develop a realistic sense of what can be achieved*—and what cannot; that is, be confident but recognize the realistic capacity of
  the organization.
- *Start from where the organization is*—that is, be fully aware of

an organization's own current state of the art and build on that base. There have been too many situations in which companies have been led unwittingly into beautifully designed, sophisticated new systems that were beyond the capacity of the organization's personnel to handle.

○ *Maintain open vertical and lateral communications.* Openness helps to allay fears. There must be a sense of trust among the followers in their managerial leaders. Change there will be—but no "games" will be played. There must be assurances that changes will be made thoughtfully and openly.

○ *Develop a "change mentality."* Achieve a sense of enthusiasm and pride that the organization is strengthening itself by making changes. Emphasize the advantages of the changes and realistically recognize and deal with any disadvantages—and there surely will be some. Plan well and carry out change in an effective, quality way. Gain the confidence of the organization that the changes can be carried out successfully without "messing up" the operation. A poorly executed change will clearly be a setback for achieving a positive change in attitude. Importantly, today's manager/leaders have to deal in fresh ways with new working relationships—becoming a customer-driven marketer, coping with new strategies, and developing a healthy attitude toward change, to name a few. In total, these represent a monumental task because they call for new strategies and the will and competence to bring about change. While some of the parts individually may be done well, in the aggregate these call for a special kind of leadership to bring them all off in a team-like, organized way.

○ *Be totally honest.* Be forthright about the possible gain from the change. Recognize the high probability of pain with the assurance that all reasonable steps will be taken to minimize the hurt to people in the organization.

To bring about meaningful change requires a great deal of technical smarts. If the leaders want to change the company, for example, to a customer-driven marketing organization, they must understand the fabric from which customer marketing is to be fashioned. They must understand the specific design of the new pattern of operations. But that by itself is insufficient. Equally important, the leaders must understand how to change attitudes and inspire people to be excited about doing things differently because it means improvement. It was said of Roger Smith, former chairman of General Motors, "Smith came to understand that real change at General Motors would not simply be an exchange of ideas or even intellectual agreement but rather he had to *get the organization to respond to his creative drive."*

The Boeing Corporation is in the throes of a challenging change experience. Boeing must strive to be the low-cost producer for the airline industry—the primary user of Boeing's commercial products. Over time the low-cost producer always has a key advantage in battling for market supremacy. Clearly many technical and quantitative improvements must be made. But the greatest challenge for Dean Thornton (the former president of the Commercial Aircraft Division) was simply to develop the will and enthusiasm throughout the organization to bring about the changes. Boeing will be no exception—change is difficult for people to accept. And creating the right attitude and desire is the ultimate call and responsibility of the manager/leader.

Jack F. Welch has brought about monumental changes in General Electric. Since he became chief executive officer, change has come fast; some have called it an upheaval. As Mr. Welch has said, he wants to shake people and say, "Wait a minute, the world's a different place." He is eliminating layers of management, streamlining the processes of management, and causing people to be more entrepreneurial. Certainly a good part of what indicates some early successes stems from the extent to which Jack Welch has breathed a new sense of urgency and drama into the organization. It will be largely his capacity to sustain this "change psyche" of his people that will determine Jack Welch's and General Electric's long-term success.

By contrast, it is interesting that John S. Reed, chairman at Citicorp, has moved cautiously to bring about change more slowly and with a much lower profile than Welch at General Electric. In fact,

Reed has worked hard to solidify his internal position of strength and in the process has enhanced the effective interdimensional cooperation of key bank officers. In essence, he is bringing about change in subtle but meaningful ways, but doing so without the seemingly "shake them up" process in the style of Jack Welch. Both approaches may well be highly successful.

There is another interesting example in Roger Smith of General Motors. He tried to bring about change that challenged the very culture of the company. He attacked the entrenched way of life at General Motors. He asked a long-time bureaucracy to become more venturesome and more entrepreneurial. It was a daring task that was necessary to tackle if General Motors was to face the Japanese head on and beat them. Roger Smith and General Motors knew that success would depend on two things: (1) the extent to which he and his people could successfully identify creative ideas for dramatically increasing General Motors' capacity to compete at low cost; and (2) the extent to which Roger Smith and his leadership team could develop a sense of new purpose and drive throughout the organization. There was a need to develop a change attitude—a need to instill in their people an excitement and a realization that with change would come real progress.

Another interesting case in point is United States Steel. Apparently David M. Roderick brought about more change during the 1980s than the corporation had experienced for many decades. He has shut down plants, drastically reduced capacity, and cut his white collar work force by over 50 percent. On the marketing/business side he has sold large pieces of assets and acquired Marathon Oil Company, which makes him a larger oil company than a steel company (at least in terms of revenue). Perhaps most significantly, he is trying to change the attitudes and culture of the company. He is attempting to move a $20 billion sales giant from a stolid, hierarchical, bureaucratic organization into one much leaner, more responsive, and above all else market and customer driven. Roderick may be undertaking one of the most difficult change challenges in business today. Indeed he has brought about much change in his eight years of leadership. He has won—and perhaps lost—some battles. But the war is still in progress and the outcome is still in question. Clearly he must make those business decisions that will over time achieve a return on investment equal to or better than the average of U.S. manufacturing companies. That is the ultimate objective of his massive changes. This will call for creative moves in both the oil and steel industries—unenviable tasks. To succeed will require some of the most astute business/market acumen he can muster. Besides that, and equally important, he must instill a sense of newfound drive and purpose in his people. It can appropriately and punningly be said that he will have to "steel" his people to the task. Roderick must bring about a new attitude, yes, a sense of thrill in his people for successfully bringing about change—that by changing, the company can win and grow. The pain will indeed be great, thus there must be a strong belief permeating the organization that under this leadership the company will succeed and in the process individuals will also succeed.

Another excellent case in point is IBM—long considered most conservative and generally not quick to change. Louis F. Gerstner, chairman and CEO, is now in the process of bringing about a significant transformation at IBM. In commenting on this, a down-the-line officer and a veteran in the company said that changing attitudes is the most difficult part of this transformation. He summarized by saying, "The change has not been an easy one and called for unique leadership skills." Few large organizations have been as successful in managing change. This is a mark of quality leadership, especially in this era of global discontinuity. Despite these successes, IBM is still in the process of climbing up the managerial leadership ladder to make their bureaucratic organization more nimble and flexible.

Few companies have mastered the art of change better than American Express. It has become the clear leader in the credit card business because of its unusual capacity to identify opportunities during this period of discontinuity and then to marshal and shift its capabilities to take advantage of the market situation. But the real secret has been its entrepreneurial leadership that can react quickly and motivate its people to take risks in a rapidly changing marketplace. Clearly its managers have made some astute decisions, particularly in the travel-related part of their business. There is no denying their splendid strategy but, equally important, their leadership has had the special skills needed to generate confidence and motivate people to accept and even enjoy the exhilaration of change. American Express's success is as much due to the qualitative aspects of its leadership to bring about a healthy change in attitude as it is to their splendid strategy and execution.

One point is clear in all of these change examples. Important as the technical aspects of change are, and indeed they are essential, the primary determinant to success will be the capacity of the leaders to create a sustaining motivation and desire within their people to bring about changes. In essence, their real leadership task is to create a will, even a desire, to bring about change throughout the organization. The final determinant of success will not be technical competence, although this is necessary; rather it will be the quality of inspired change leadership.

13 ARE LEADERS BORN OR MADE?

That's really not the right question. They are both born and made—but more made than born.

The answer is both. A reasonably intelligent person with adequate drive and a natural capacity to relate to people can develop (and be developed) into a competent manager/leader.

To the extent a leader is born, there are some very basic elements of character and personality that will importantly shape—and yes, limit or enhance—the quality and extent of ultimate leadership performance. These might include such fundamental qualities as endurance, integrity, drive, desire, an inner sense of responsibility, and natural sensitivity to people. Where these are lacking it is difficult—if not impossible—to develop them in adulthood. Conversely, where these kinds of personality and character traits are present there is a foundation for developing leadership. The important point here is to recognize that many people have inherited the basic raw material but never have had the opportunity or do not take the opportunity to develop or be developed. By this I mean that the person with potential may never be thrust into a position where the opportunity to lead is present. For example, to steal from and paraphrase an old saying, "To always sail on a calm sea may not create a great captain." Expressed another way, it was adversity that undoubtedly motivated David to create and sing the Psalms. Then, too, the person with basic potential may never enjoy the benefit of a mentor and thus languish without truly developing.

It is equally true that where basic traits of character and personality are lacking the possibility of achieving success as a manager/

leader are slim. Regardless of whether such a person has a mentor, or is thrown into a situation demanding leadership, or even both of these, emerging as an effective manager/leader is highly doubtful. The bottom line is simply that a reasonably intelligent person with adequate drive and a natural capacity to relate to people can develop (or be developed) into a competent manager/leader.

Prior to World War II there were but few training or development courses for manager/leaders in the United States, and this was true for the rest of the western world. Following the war our major corporations faced enormous challenges concerning how to effectively manage the explosion in the growth of our industrial society. To fill the need, management turned its attention and talents to a more organized approach to growing new manager/leaders. Our universities and particularly the graduate schools of business got into the act. Since 1950 we have turned out a whole new generation of manager/leaders on a scale unprecedented in our history. Lawrence Appley, past leader of the American Management Association (who did much to promote training and development of managers), considered this organized effort to develop managers on a professional basis to be one of the most remarkable developments in our society in the second half of the twentieth century. Indeed it has been. The United States has been successful in developing legions of new manager/leaders, and I say this in the face of the charge that business schools do not develop leaders. While I quarrel some with today's business school curriculum that focuses so much on analysis and technique, I would still enthusiastically credit them with helping talented people along the path to leadership.

First, there was an acute need to develop manager/leaders; and of course it is need or wants that drive our industrial engine. Because we needed manager/leaders, we were driven to develop them. Second, we mustered our skills and resources to concentrate on the task of human development. Business management, universities, and consultants— to name a few—converged on the problem. Individuals gave more time and attention to the problem, particularly through on-the-job training and coaching (much like a modern day coach helps to grow his athletes). Other parts of our society have also gotten into the act. For example, hospitals are training professional administrators to help manage their complex institutions. And we are turning out over sixty thousand MBAs each year in this country alone.

Clearly, there is overwhelming evidence that we can do much on an organized basis to nurture and hasten the growth of quality manager/leaders. To deny this truth would be too frightening to accept. There are three important factors we must keep in mind above all else. First, there are more people with leadership potential than we realize. This is not a small, elitist group of "superb people," but probably a larger portion of our population than we suspect. Second, we must do a more intelligent and courageous job of seeking out and encouraging those with the appropriate potential. We must detect some special quality or qualities such as motivation, a sense of vision, strength of character, emotional stability, a high sense of responsibility, and capacity to influence, to suggest a few vital and fundamental building traits. And third, we can recognize that we need manager/leaders at all levels in our society. We are not just talking about chairmen, presidents, and vice presidents. We are not just talking about a Bismarck, a Douglas MacArthur, or a Winston Churchill. We need leaders over a few and over many. One of the finest examples of leadership I ever witnessed was that of a squad leader in an infantry company during World War II. This leader, a corporal, had guts, was an extremely tough trainer and disciplinarian, absolutely fair, knew his business, and was dead-level honest. A superb leader over a squad of twelve men, and perhaps he could have led a platoon (four squads), but I think he would have been lost trying to lead an infantry company (four platoons). It is important therefore to recognize that we must seek out and develop competent manager/leaders to place over tens, fifties, hundreds, and thousands—that the corporal leading the squad is as vital a part of our managerial leadership fabric as is the corporate vice president of marketing, the university president, the hospital administrator, the city mayor, or even the supervisor of the sanitation crew (which may well become a top priority in the critical problem of waste disposal and recycling).

At the risk of repeating a point made in an earlier chapter, many writers and thinkers in the field of the behavioral sciences have been critical by saying that we are creating managers and not leaders. This, I think, is a misreading of the truth. What we are creating are people who have a mixture of both managerial and leadership skills and attributes. And we need both managers and leaders. However, there is reason indeed for some concern. In our management development programs—whether university, corporate, or any other—we tend to emphasize manager-type skills. I am particularly sensitive to the charges against our graduate business schools. The attackers believe that the business schools concentrate almost solely on technique, analysis, and process, that the MBA student thinks too singularly about financial analysis, market research, or how to build mathematical models. In brief, the management school graduate tends to learn "management by the numbers." The attackers point out that while knowledge and techniques will be useful, in fact vital, what will eventually cause the MBA to be truly successful and make a significant contribution will be demonstrated ability to get meaningful things done through people in an organization—that is, to lead through other leaders.

Coming back to my opening point, leaders are partially born and partially made. Few are truly natural-born leaders. Most of our manager/leaders are bent and shaped by experience, the need to respond to a challenge and often to a leader who had the ability and desire to help create another leader. But I think in the final analysis the individual mostly learns to become a leader by leading and that much of the action is self-generated.

As an interesting personal example, I was taught and learned a great lesson in leadership that has remained with me all of my adult life. Early in my military career I lived through a challenging experience that many manager/leaders in all types of organizations face repeatedly over their careers. My unforgettable experience occurred on my first duty assignment after being commissioned a second lieutenant in the Army during World War II. I know I was young—I shaved twice a week even if I didn't need it. I was a total rookie, never having served in an active military organization. My first assignment was as a platoon lieutenant commanding one sergeant, four corporals, and some sixty soldiers of private rank. When I arrived to take over my new, and first, command duties, the sergeant and four corporals came forth to meet me with a smart salute while standing at stiff attention until I gave the order, "At ease, men." I was startled and in some shock when I realized that my five noncommissioned officers (one sergeant and four corporals) were probably twenty years older than I and (as I knew from their records) all five had fifteen or more years' experience in the regular army.

I knew I was really in a lot of trouble—I had never commanded troops and in the process I had to command a sergeant and four corporals who knew the military inside and out. I knew that if they wanted to they could "chew me up and spit me out" several times a day. Fortunately I remembered the advice of a wise colonel who commanded us in officers' candidate school. To carry out the colonel's advice I invited the five noncommissioned officers to join me at the Post Exchange (restaurant and bar). We spent three hours drinking Cokes and beer and talking about "managing a platoon." I started the conversation by reminding them that I had never commanded a platoon but I was sent there to do a job and I desperately wanted to become an excellent officer. I sincerely asked the sergeant and corporals if they would take me under their care and teach me how to be a great officer. I promised to be a quick learner. And we all agreed that this "coaching" had to be done in a way that would build me up in the eyes of the troops.

We all shook hands across the table and the sergeant, speaking for himself and the corporals, said that they would count it a privilege to work with me and to make ours the first platoon in the battalion. Then for two hours they reviewed the important things I was supposed to do as the platoon commander. And each evening after the day's work with the troops the six of us would meet in my quarters and they would critique my performance for the day. In just a few short weeks my officership performance was shaped and reshaped. They were tough but thoughtful and helpful.

Sometime later we won the distinction of being the best platoon in the battalion, and I got high ratings on my officer evaluation. But the greatest joy came some months later when the sergeant told me that he and the four corporals had never grown so much in confidence and stature as when they taught their lieutenant how to be a great officer. As he said, the teachers learned the most. And it was not until many years later that I realized that my noncommissioned officers had given me a great lesson in how to be a "Servant Leader." Vivid memories of that experience have remained with me over the years. From that lesson I have counseled many young men and women as they newly go into managerial positions to seek out ideas and help particularly from the long service people whom they will have the challenge and privilege to manage and lead. This counsel is particularly meaningful and useful to young MBAs who go out into industry to become managers over people who will be senior both in age and years of experience in the organization the MBA is about to lead.

However, it is vital, I think, to our future to always remember the important role that the mentor can play. Harkening back to Plutarch's *Lives,* we recall the marvelous lessons in leadership that Fabius with great wisdom administered to Minucius. Minucius suffered a stunning defeat by Hannibal because of the former's overconfidence and impetuosity. Despite the defeat, Fabius, the supreme commander, recognized great potential. So instead of sending him back to Rome in disgrace he gave Minucius another chance. Fabius administered his mentorship in a way that reformed and reshaped Minucius, who could have been "lost," into a splendid military commander. It must always be remembered that the highest and noblest calling to a manager/leader is to help create a new leader—and not necessarily in his/her own image.

Theodore Roosevelt represents a telling example of a great leader who was hardly born a leader but rather worked hard to develop his natural gifts. Roosevelt also inherited some natural disadvantages. He was small of stature, not physically strong, and had an uncommanding voice. He drove himself to overcome these natural drawbacks. In the process he developed an obsession to lead and command. Most importantly, he developed a rugged, restless constitution that enabled him to outwork and inspire other men to action. As the historians have already concluded, Theodore Roosevelt was largely a leader of his own creation. He was a living example that, given some basic raw material, a man or woman can by sheer force of determination and will develop into a leader. Roosevelt was obviously born with ambition, a desire to achieve, and some kind of innate capacity to relate to people. But it was a deep-seated determination and drive that shaped his capacity to manage and lead. He was more made than born. Yes, that is the answer—leaders are part born and part made—but more, and more effectively, made.

It is not the lot of the leader to be served but rather his/her privilege to serve. Ich Dien *appears prominently on the crest of the Prince of Wales. It says, so simply, "I serve." Putting that concept into practice is the basis for developing the servant leader concept.*

Developing the qualities of the servant leader is difficult because the servant leader must be more selfless than selfish. The servant leader is one who has followers whom he/she helps to grow in stature, capacity, or in some way contributes to building them into more useful and satisfied people. As the Good Book says, "If anyone would be first, he must be servant of all." Not all successful manager/leaders ever become true servant leaders. Indeed, there are cases in corporate life where a successful manager "takes from his people" and in the process does relatively little to build them, just as there are farmers who totally devastate the soil. However, there is growing evidence that today's mature manager/leaders and those of tomorrow must more and more face up to the high demands of being servant leaders. Expressed in a most forceful way, the leader is the shepherd of the flock. He/she "washes their feet" as well as applies the whip. The true leader has a strong sense of caring for his troops. He/she blends compassion and force.

The true servant leaders follow St. Paul's concept, which I paraphrase: To give and to grow and to build and never in the leader's own striving to cause another to stumble. The servant leader is one with a high sense of humanity. As Shakespeare put it, "He must have the power to hurt and yet will do none." In effect, the leader by definition has the power to hurt, yet the mature servant leader will rarely if ever use that power. Indeed it is difficult to become a true servant leader because essentially one must be truly unselfish.

Like the shepherd of the flock, the leader is accessible to his/her people. The Emperor Hadrian, early in the second century when he ruled much of the civilized world, was riding into Rome in his chariot. An old woman blocked his path and asked him to hear her grievance. Hadrian brushed her aside, saying he was too busy. "Then you're too busy to be Emperor," she called after him. Whereupon he halted his chariot and heard her out.

The servant leader can learn much from the example of the shepherd of antiquity. The true shepherd prepared the pasture before the sheep entered the field. In essence the shepherd, the leader, goes before to make sure the way is safe—safe from snakes, lions, or even thistles that could harm the sheep's mouth. In brief he/she leads from the front, he/she goes before his/her troops, he/she does not tag along in the rear.

If we are to have followers who follow freely and willingly, they must believe that the leader has interest in and affection for them. The supreme test is that the true leader makes his/her followers better than they would otherwise have been. There must be some element or sense of life in high-quality leadership, for without this quality of the servant leader, leadership can appear to be—and in fact becomes —self-serving and selfishly motivated.

Being the servant leader is further difficult because it requires an unusual tolerance for imperfection. This does not mean accepting less than high-quality effort, but rather an honest realization that "God made more slow people than fast people," that organizations are not made up of angels but that a leader's task is often to deal with the imperfections that he/she has to work with and lead the half-people that we are. Striving for perfection is frustrating; striving for excellence can be gratifying.

Being the manager/leader means leading people in such a way that they grow in their capacity to produce because of the leader. When the leader demands more from people, he/she has a responsibility to help increase his/her people's capacity to produce. We might all ponder over the tough, self-examining question: "Who has truly grown under me and what role did I play?"

The ultimate test of a good leader is to grow another good leader and in the process expand the capacity of followers to contribute to the organization. And finally, probably the most thrilling and satisfying experience in management is to grow another person—to increase another's capacity and desire to contribute.

I recall so vividly back in August 1942 listening to the words of wisdom of a general who was speaking to a group of newly commissioned second lieutenants, of whom I was one. After welcoming us to the ranks of officership he gave a short orientation speech about life as an army officer during wartime. One comment I shall never forget. He told us to always, "Feed your troops—and they will fight like hell for you. But I don't mean just feed the belly, although that is important. I also mean to feed the mind, the heart, and the spirit. Grow the total soldier." I have never forgotten his admonition. Often I have advised managers to *grow the total person*. Returning again to my leadership experiences in World War II, I still recall so vividly the exhortation of our division commanding general. His key message, which holds true at any time in any place, was simply, "Serve your troops first that you may command them better."

During a recent trip to England, I observed many times the crest of Charles, the Prince of Wales. On his crest appear these two German words, *Ich Dien,* meaning "I serve." And the extent to which he truly lives that motto will determine to a large extent his success in the years ahead. Donald Burr, the dynamic and often controversial founder and former chief executive officer of People Express, summed up his own leadership philosophy by saying, "You don't just want to make a buck. You want people to become better people." (Even with that noble philosophy his organization failed, demonstrating that leadership is complex and requires more than a single great quality.) By that I think Burr was saying that it is the role of the leader to both serve as well as lead. In fact, it is by serving that the leader shapes his/her leadership. And it is by making people better—by increasing their capacity to perform—that the leader can multiply the power of the entire organization and truly magnify his/her own power and effectiveness.

David R. Holmes, CEO of Reynolds & Reynolds, speaks of a deep commitment and involvement with his organization and its people. He is always visible, he is there among his people. They know his involvement is for real. He is totally dedicated to making Reynolds & Reynolds a high-performing information technology organization. His people know this.

A student of leadership recently said that the first requirement of leadership is to "be there." By this I believe he meant that the leader should be where the action is. To see and feel the presence of the manager/leader in the midst of a tough situation is reassuring. The impact of leadership is a necessary ingredient and personal presence among your people is often the most powerful way to reinforce this. I recall a leadership speech I heard some years ago. The speaker was saying that there are three requirements to being an achiever. First was simply to be there—to be there particularly when needed. Second was to be on time, which to him meant to be early, ready for action. Third was to be prepared—to have done your homework. While overly simplistic, these three precepts do emphasize the importance of being present in order to impact the result.

An incident from Joseph Conrad's book *Typhoon* emphasizes the power of the leader's presence. Conrad writes: "Jukes was uncritically glad to have his captain at hand. It relieved him as though that man had, by simply coming on deck, taken at once most of the gale's weight upon his shoulders. Such is the prestige, the privilege, and the burden of command."

One of the finest servant leaders I have ever known was an infantry captain I served under who was training us back in the summer of 1941 for combat in the war which broke out a few months later. This captain was trained in the regular army; he was incredibly tough on us and demanded the utmost in discipline and performance, and many of us, unused to military life, characterized him as rough and tough, unreasonably harsh, and almost cruel. At first most of us "hated his guts!" But later we learned that he had only two objectives and they were simple but not necessarily easy to achieve: "To make you guys the best fighters in the world and most important to increase your chances of coming back home alive and well." He drove us relentlessly but all of us knew that he really cared for us and that everything he did was to make us more capable to fight and defend ourselves. The captain could have gotten by with demanding less from us and it would have meant less work for him. But he had a compelling desire to help us become the best, to come out a winner and stay alive. He demonstrated the true mark of the servant leader.

The ultimate test of the servant leader is to work constructively with the half-people who are part of all organizations. The real secret to building a winning organization is to be able to forge an effective team from the imperfect people by raising them up to be bigger than they otherwise might have been—to increase individually and collectively their power to perform. Doing that is the stamp of the servant leader.

The true servant leader has a sense of love toward his/her people, and they know it. Sun Tzu, the fifth century B.C. Chinese warlord told his commanders, "Treat your soldiers like your own beloved son and they will walk through the valley of death with you."

We only need to examine the lives of great leaders from the past. Alexander, Caesar, Charlemagne, Lincoln, or Churchill—to realize that styles vary widely. Obviously, many different styles work. What is important is that a leader's style be an honest reflection of what the person really is. The style must be genuine.

Styles of leadership have always fascinated historians. For centuries chroniclers as well as military men have mused on the generalship of such greats as Hannibal, Alexander, and Napoleon. Brilliant strategists and tacticians—all three, but varying in leadership styles. In fact, there are probably as many styles of leadership as there are leaders. Those who manage the affairs of other men display supremely individualistic traits. In our own experience, at one time or another, each of us may have met with counterparts of classic models, present-day descendants exhibiting the bravado of a Genghis Khan, the calm mastery of a Caesar, the drive and purpose of a Bismarck, the dignity and statesmanlike qualities of a Robert E. Lee, or the eloquence and valor of a Churchill.

In every field of action successful styles may vary widely. To cite two military examples, allied forces moved into Europe during World War II under widely varied styles of command. There was the bold and fiery direction of General George S. Patton in contrast to the quietly effective leadership of General Omar Bradley. Similarly, the calm overview of Supreme Allied Commander Dwight D. Eisenhower balanced the flamboyant style of the British Field Marshall General Montgomery. All of these commanders scored repeated victories, each pursuing his goals in his own distinctive style.

Another fascinating example takes us back to the Punic Wars and the glory days of Rome. Two leaders of special interest were Marcellus, five times consul of the Romans, and Fabius Maximus, also a consul for many years. Both men were political leaders who also led legions of Roman soldiers against Hannibal the Carthaginian, who had become the scourge of Italy and was deeply feared in Rome. Fabius was a soldier leader of great integrity and wisdom whose style was shaped by extreme caution and reluctance to risk slugging it out with the enemy. He did not want to "put it all on the line." It was his style to keep his enemy constantly on the move, never quite engaging him and hoping over time to simply wear him out. Marcellus by contrast had a style dominated by boldness. He had a burning desire and the matching bravado to quickly engage and "whip" the enemy. As we are told in Plutarch's *Lives,* the Roman Senate sent out both consul generals hoping to combine Marcellus's boldness and Fabius's caution, to temper the one by the other. It is interesting that Hannibal feared each of these two Roman leaders more than any others because each of their styles proved effective and difficult for the Carthaginian enemy to cope with.

Style is important because it so clearly affects how followers perceive leaders. Style is the way in which leadership is presented. Style impacts greatly how followers view the leaders. As such, it shapes how one follows. The practice of followership would vary between the followers of Patton and of Bradley. Expressed another way, the substance of the leader shapes his perception, that is, how he is viewed. In turn, perception shapes substance. As Pygmalion suggested, the way we are perceived shapes our performance. Style then is the sum total of how the leader presents himself/herself to his/her followers.

Leadership style has many dimensions. It is not easily categorized. It is too multifaceted to be described by a number or a ranking (9 to 1 or 1 to 9). Some describe variations in style by depicting someone as production-oriented or another as people-oriented. Some are viewed as authoritarian and others as being more participative. However, there are other more descriptive, meaningful, and qualitative ways to examine the anatomy of leadership style. Here are a few that add richness to any delineation of leadership styles.

1. *Attitude toward change.* Attitude toward change tells much about style. Coping with change is a leader's major challenge. How he/she copes with this does much to shape his/her style and frames how his/her followers will respond. Most leaders of any degree of maturity recognize the need to bring about change and improvement and in the process to help transform the organization. Despite this general recognition, leaders vary greatly in their capacity to handle change. Some tend to resist it, others even seek it out, and most fall in between. This attitude on change—whatever it is—does much to condition the response of the organization.

2. *Extent of participative management.* This second element of style deals with the extent to which the leader leads through subleaders or tends to hold the major action to himself. Is the leader's style one of extensive delegation or heavy involvement in the decisions and actions throughout the organization? In describing their styles, critics have said that President Ronald Reagan delegated too freely and was not hands-on enough. President Jimmy Carter, on the other hand, held on too tightly and restricted others from making significant contributions. This comparison does much to delineate the styles of these two leaders.

3. *Use of authority.* The way a leader acquires and uses authority is always a distinguishing feature of style. Some leaders use authority sparingly and depend more on persuasion, logic, or the fact that followers like and respect the leader and want to please by compliance. This is the quiet exercise of authority or command. This kind of exercise of authority is difficult to achieve because it requires a leader of considerable inner strength to bring it off effectively. Other leaders push their authority as a means of getting important things done. Lyndon

Johnson, for example, was a leader who would use all his legitimate authority and push for more. He flaunted presidential authority almost to the point of perceived arrogance. Franklin Delano Roosevelt also pushed outward the bounds of presidential authority. He did it with a degree of sophistication and class that did not smack of arrogance. Yet he was clearly bold in his use of power. Carter and Ford were more temperate in their use of presidential power and authority. Both of them were so preoccupied with returning trust to the Oval Office that they were understandably judicious in their use of power. Mr. Clinton has a boldness in his use of presidential power, but he does it with an adroitness that does not smack of arrogance. Each of their styles was and is partly shaped by historical events, yet the way each used authority was/is also a reflection of the individual. The "bully" Lyndon Johnson would naturally exercise authority more aggressively than the "love in his heart" Jimmy Carter. Clearly authority is a necessary ingredient to maintaining leadership. However, the way it is used can do much to make or unmake the leader. Handling authority (or power) is a potent weapon for achievement but like an explosive it must be handled with wisdom and maturity. Nothing says more about the true class of a leader than when he or she can handle authority with purpose and compassion.

4. *Handling crises and stress.* Nothing so richly paints a picture of a leader's style and image as his/her reaction to stress and conflict. The degree to which a leader has composure under fire says much about the "mark of the leader." Composure under fire by the leader instills a sense of calm and confidence in the minds of followers that acts to exhilarate. In contrast, a style that erupts and shows anger or frustration under fire can smother the spirit of followers.

5. *Decision-making process.* This is one of the critical tests of leadership skill, and a very apparent delineator of style. Making

decisions or having them made (or passing them by) is the *raison d'etre* of the leader. Making decisions is both art and science and may be more art. They rarely should be made in haste and usually should not be delayed or prolonged. Sometimes they should be made in consensus—sometimes on a solitary basis. They require a blend of fact and judgment. There is no one way to do it all the time. The process by which the leader blends art and science to make wise decisions tells much about both his/her style and maturity. And the delivery or presentation of his/her decision-making style fills the organization with confidence and comfort or fear and frustration.

6. *Demands and expectations.* The demands and expectations that the leader places on the organization and himself do much to set the tone and fiber of the organization. This element of style suggests how hard the leader will push, how fast the organization will go, and the minimum performance it will accept. Organizations like General Electric and IBM and Cummins Engine push executives to set high standards, make tough evaluations against those standards and replace mediocrity. Conversely, other leaders may appeal for improved performance but do not take tough action when performance falters. There is no single way to get high quality performance. But an important element of leadership style is the approach taken to setting performance standards, evaluating results, and the follow-up action taken.

To return to an earlier point, delineating leadership style is not a simple task. Many elements make up style—it has many dimensions. I have suggested six:

○ Attitude toward change
○ Extent of participative management
○ Use of authority

- Handling crises and stress
- Decision-making process
- Demands and expectations

And there could be others, but these are sufficient to demonstrate the many dimensions to style. It is also vital to recognize that no single style is *the* style. Just the six dimensions I have mentioned offer in combination limitless style permutations. There is great risk that a leader may try to copy style from some other leader, known either from a personal experience or from history. Much can be learned from history or other successful leaders. But there is a germ of truth that is the bottom line—the lesson we should take away from this chapter on style. Here it is:

> *The ultimate expression of style—what a leader does and the way a leader is perceived to lead—must be a genuine reflection of what the leader really is. Style must be genuine and for real. The leader's style must be an honest reflection of what he/she really is. The leader must be what he/she pretends to be. There must be true consistency between what the leader is and the image he/she attempts to project.*

16 LEADING THROUGH OTHER LEADERS: DELEGATING RESPONSIBILITY AND NURTURING PARTICIPATORY LEADERSHIP

Moses learned the dramatic lesson over thirty-five hundred years ago that he had to lead through subleaders. Inspired as he was, he had to learn that he could not do it alone. He needed to unleash the power of his people.

Leading through other leaders is the leader's most difficult and yet most important task. His/her purpose in life is to get meaningful things done through people. This is the fundamental test of a leader —can he/she motivate and lead through subleaders? Increasingly, accomplishing this has demanded that people down the line be included more and more in the action if they are to be effective producers and contributors. The task then is how to involve the people in an organization in the managing process without losing control, direction, and the desired rate of thrust. Some years ago Thomas J. Watson, Jr., then chairman of IBM, made the timeless comment that "the real difference between success and failure in a corporation can very often be traced to the question of how well the organization brings out the great energies and talents of its people." *Expressed another way, it is the capacity to unleash the power of your people that determines the ultimate success of a leader and the organization.*

The story of Moses as told to us in the eighteenth chapter of Exodus shows how he struggled in 1400 B.C. with the problem of delegation and participation. Jethro, the Midian priest, spoke to Moses:

"Why do you sit alone and all the people stand about you from morning until evening? What you are doing is not good. You and the people with you will wear themselves out, for the thing is too heavy for you. You are not able to perform it alone.

107

"Listen and I will give counsel. You shall teach them the statutes and make them know the way in which they must walk and what they must do.

"Moreover, choose able men from all the people—men who are trustworthy and who hate a bribe—and place such men over the people as rulers of thousands, of hundreds, of fifties, and of tens. And let them rule the people at all times, every great matter they shall bring to you, but any small matter they shall decide themselves. So it will be easier for you and they shall share the burden with you. So Moses gave heed and did all Jethro said."

Despite his great motivation, his sense of mission, and his dedication to great causes, Moses was unable to move his people because he did not lead through other leaders and in the process he stifled initiative and involvement in the managing process. Fortunately, he was counseled before it was too late on how to delegate and multiply the effectiveness of his leadership by involving subleaders—and thus he saved the Israelite nation. The point of the story is simply to recognize that delegation of decision making, participative management, and leading through other leaders are vital to increasing the total power of the leader and the organization. In essence the whole organization as a result can get more things done—its accomplishments are magnified. However, delegating and involving others runs naturally against the grain of many leaders or potential leaders because by their very nature they desire and enjoy making decisions themselves. Men and women become leaders because they demonstrate initiative, a certain verve, and by their recognized capacity to take action. And these are the most demonstrable characteristics and often outshine their less showy skills of thinking, problem analysis, and developing the capacity of others to act. However, the whole purpose of an organization is to provide the vehicle by which greater power can be unleashed down through and across the organization and thus create more decision makers—and more doers—giving the total enterprise greater capacity to move forward. The executive manager/leader must get down-the-line managers meaningfully involved in determining objectives, developing action programs and making decisions of significance.

Unfortunately, too many top managements equate delegative and participatory management with weakness; actually the reverse is true. It takes strong top managers to bring about effective delegation and participative management. It means setting demanding objectives in which the widest number of managers participate and, in the process, each makes personal commitment and contribution. And this must be followed by an appraisal of their performances against the pre-established standards.

It is the weak or unimaginative manager/leader who will, through fear or inability to develop a managing process, hold most of the action to himself, resulting in little contribution by the bulk of down-the-line managers. Too often manager/leaders are so busy making decisions that they fail to develop or use a process by which others can make decisions and take action—in effect, they do not realize the multiplying power that comes from having more decision makers. Without broad participation—held together by an ordered process—the total organization will never achieve its fullest power. But that is the role of the leader.

There can be a multiplying power in increasing the number of decision makers. In any organization of even moderate size, hundreds —yes, thousands—of decisions must be made daily to carry out its business. These decisions of course represent a wide spectrum of importance or impact on the totality of the organization—the key point is that they must be made and implemented. Similar to the situation of Moses and his people the decision-making process in an organization must be spread across a wide spectrum of the management both horizontally and vertically—throughout the organization. In a sense each decision maker is a power cell of varying size and intensity and taken together they represent a powerful source of decision-making energy and accomplishment. Practicing this kind of managerial leadership results in leading through other leaders. This accomplishes two major important purposes.

First, it simply enables the organization to get more done. The people in the organization do not have "to stand around from morning until night" waiting for decisions. In essence the organization is more productive—it gets more done and moves ahead faster. Second, this kind of managerial leadership is a good spawning ground for nurturing strong future leaders. To the extent that this type of participative management gives down-the-line people the chance to be exposed to the evolution of decisions and their implementation, it can be a vital force for creating new leaders. This is not to suggest that everybody gets together and jointly makes the decisions. Roger Smith, former chairman of General Motors, expressed this idea well when he said, "Give me your ideas and I'll decide." This will work to the extent that the giver of the idea has some sense that the ideas offered can sometimes make a difference. Indeed the process of seeking ideas has to be genuine. If it is a hollow exercise it will soon be found out and labeled dishonest—a sham. In General Motors' experience there has developed a good give and take process nurtured by an openness and willingness to change and try new ideas. The willingness to frankly say that an idea is "no good" as well as "good" is vital to making the process believable. If it in any way smacks of being a phony exercise the real value is lost. If there is going to be participation it should be meaningful but never to the extent that the leader loses control and respect—neither the leaders or followers would want it that way.

Effective participatory management/leadership when practiced at its highest level really means that leaders are leading through other leaders. Leadership does not and should not exist only at the top. A leader extends his/her effectiveness and power not by holding everything to himself but by growing other subleaders to make decisions and motivate followers at all levels throughout the organization. As Moses fortunately learned before it was too late, he too had to lead through other leaders by sharing with them the burdens of governing his people. *The ultimate achievement of the great leader is the degree to which he/she creates subleaders and then leads through them.* The leadership philosophy of President Reagan (particularly in his first term) presses home this point. He strongly believed and practiced the principle of surrounding himself with good people, delegating authority, and not interfering as long as his basic policy was being carried out. That is the supreme way to unleash the power of the organization. That is what organizing and accomplishment are all about, leading through other leaders—unleashing the power of your people and in the process growing more managerial leadership talent.

While it is overly simplistic, the leader has two basic responsibilities. First is to keep the operation viable and competitive today. Second is to build new manager/leaders who can take the organization successfully into the future. There are other responsibilities, but these two are at the core.

One of the most vital needs in any organization is to ensure its continuity. Someone succinctly summed up the manager/leader's task in this simple way: "To do well the job today and to provide new leaders for tomorrow." The task of developing the new leaders can be broken down into the following steps.

- *Identify those with high potential.* Selection is a critical ingredient in developing new leaders. It requires identifying individuals with basic leadership qualities or raw materials such as motivation, judgment, and energy, which the future leader must possess and which no one else can teach him. This basic raw material is more God-given than developed, although even those who have it must nurture it.
- *Set demanding expectations for potential leaders.* Expect excellence—demand much. The tone and drive of any organization is shaped by the expectation levels set by its leaders. *No organization or group of individuals achieves greatness unless there is a restless desire for excellence—unless demands and expectations are high—unless great demands are made.*
- *Provide resources and ideas.* To demand excellence is not enough. The mature leader must support high demands by providing his/

113

her subordinates with resources and ideas, thoughtful direction, sufficient manpower, and selective coaching. The test of a good manager/leader is not just how much he/she demands, but rather the ability to increase the capacity of his/her people to produce more in order to reach higher standards of performance.

○ *Help subordinates set self-improvement programs.* One of the most valuable things a leader can do is to help subordinates on an individual basis set self-improvement objectives and establish programs and interim targets for achieving the improvements. Together the senior and subordinate leaders should identify the major areas for concentration, those areas of vital importance to *both the individual's growth and the organization's mission.* And together they should develop a program for action and mount a disciplined follow-up. In this way the thoughtful leader can do much to guide, inspire, coach, and develop his/ her subordinates. In the process, he/she will be expanding his/ her own competence—for *no leader grows unless he/she helps others to grow.*

○ *Coach on a selective, individual basis.* Personal attention and counseling can be an invaluable development tool when used in the spirit of building. The most useful approach is to offer guidance immediately following an important event, while the experience is fresh, showing in specific ways what could have been done differently and *how.* The suggestions should be concrete and the younger leader should thoroughly understand them and the importance of change where it will bring more productive results.

○ *Measure results and provide feedback.* The developing manager needs a periodic and forthright review of his/her progress, indicating where he/she has done well and where improvement will make a significant difference. It is important to concentrate on a few important improvement opportunities and avoid nitpicking. Such feedback on performance should be made against preestablished and mutually understood objectives, all part of a growth program.

○ *Put managers to work.* Make use of subordinates, particularly calling on their strengths. Unless a manager is used, that is, put to work, he or she will not grow; like a muscle that is unused will become flabby and atrophy. It makes the most sense when putting developing managers to work to build on their strengths rather than to be excessively preoccupied with weaknesses and trying to correct them.

At the heart of effective development of subordinates is the willingness and capacity of the manager/leader to delegate. We all learn by doing; thus the manager/leader learns by actually managing and leading. However, delegation of responsibility, decision making, and authority is one of the most difficult things a manager/leader is called upon to do. It is probably one of the poorest practiced of the many arts of leadership. Because it is so vital for manager/leaders to delegate, to share the managerial/leadership burden, it is important that we examine the issue of delegation and why it is often done so ineffectively. Clearly delegation involves risk to the organization and particularly to the executive who is doing the delegating. Let's explore the anatomy of delegation further and highlight some of its difficulties.

1. First, executives generally like to personally make decisions—it is challenging and fun and brings with it a sense of power. In this regard it is tough to give up decision making to a subordinate.
2. Second, executives often have not examined their own jobs carefully enough to identify the high-leverage decisions and activities they must hold to themselves while at the same time recognizing the lesser critical decisions and areas they could appropriately relinquish to their subleaders.
3. Third, there is often present a basic fear that by delegation the individual manager/leader becomes more vulnerable to the uncertainties of the future. After all, who can make better decisions than the leader him- or herself?

4. The manager/leader may lose control through delegation, particularly if he/she does not have an effective feedback system to tell quickly if a subordinate's actions are on target or not or if he/she is unsure of his/her own job.

Putting subleaders to work by delegating decision-making authority is perhaps the highest responsibility and privilege of the manager/ leader. Until the leader does this intelligently and courageously, those under him or her cannot grow and develop into new manager/leaders.

When we stop growing we start to die. Growing is the quality that makes leaders exciting and inspiring to follow.

Personal growth is at the very heart of effective managerial leadership. One of the great hazards of corporate life is managerial stagnation. The criteria against which we are being judged are becoming ever more demanding. The targets we are shooting at are always moving. The pressures on leaders to produce and excel will intensify. In the face of this too many leaders knowingly or unknowingly are vegetating.

What does this demand of us? We must as leaders read—listen—observe—study—and, most importantly, intelligently apply our ideas and wisdom. This means keeping the mind constantly alert to identify principles and ideas, relate them to one's own life and work experience, and then actually put them into practice. It is not a question of memorizing facts but of using new knowledge to shape our lives. Over time, putting knowledge into action enriches our experiences and adds to our wisdom.

I would admonish the growing manager/leader to expand his/her horizons, to continually nurture his/her capacity to think and reason. There is a need to constantly develop one's mental equipment. Read, listen, observe, be alive to the events surrounding you. There is a continuing need—and in fact a joy—to replenish one's well of ideas, knowledge, and experience. As the old Chinese proverb says, "Taking out without putting in soon comes to the bottom." My former firm, McKinsey & Company, lives by an important but simple creed: "Grow or go."

However, knowledge is not power, it is only potential power. The important task is to put knowledge to effective and constructive use in your life—that is, to apply the lessons gained from knowledge and experience to your own life and work and the operations of your organization to make them more effective. This point is forcefully brought home by the experience of the minister who one Sunday delivered a sermon that was well received by his congregation. In fact, one parishioner, Mr. Brown, as he greeted the minister at the conclusion of the service said, "Reverend, that was the greatest sermon I ever heard." The following Sunday as they were greeting each other the minister again thanked Mr. Brown for his kind words of praise the previous Sunday. The minister then asked, "Mr. Brown, if you thought my sermon was great, tell me, did it influence your life this past week, that is, did you do any good deeds that you might not have done had you not heard my sermon?" Mr. Brown was speechless and embarrassed. Unfortunately, he failed to recognize that to truly grow demands that we extract important principles and ideas from all we hear and see and then apply each to the betterment of our own lives and in the process impact positively on others. There is too much effort directed to gaining knowledge for the sake of knowledge. The real crux in personal development is to use newly gained knowledge and ideas to reshape our own approaches, attitudes, and practices. I remember well the words from a recent sermon by the Reverend Dr. Kenneth Hindman delivered in Lake Forest, Illinois. In speaking about a game plan for winning he said, "All of us need to train, to study, to think, and to stretch." This is a great recipe for striving for leadership excellence.

One of the tragedies in today's organizations is the excessive amount of managerial obsolescence. Too many managers are unable to cope with the increased demands placed upon them by the rapid changes going on in markets, technology, and socioeconomic shifts. There is no simple anodyne for managerial obsolescence. Overcoming it requires vigilance, discipline, and the will to learn new ways and change attitudes.

So as we read, listen, observe, and study we must try to identify and extract important lessons, concepts, or principles and relate them to our own life situations to determine where to put that knowledge to effective and constructive use. However, wisdom does not come at once. It is the accumulation of knowledge and experience that can evolve into wisdom. In brief, the leader seeks knowledge and new ideas and most importantly acts on them to help his/her own organization grow—and in the process grows himself, not instantly but continually over time.

A word about growth and age. It is generally believed that as we get older it becomes increasingly difficult and perhaps not possible to study and learn effectively. That, I believe, is pure myth. In fact, new evidence points to the growth of new brain cells even late in life. Neuroscientists are finding more neural flexibility in old age than we had imagined. It is now believed pretty much beyond doubt that the brain continues to bloom if stimulated by a rich environment and cerebral exercise. W. Clement Stone, founder and long time chairman of Combined International Corporation (now Aon) maintains that he never felt more intellectually active and competent than he did during his eighty-fifth year. His positive mental attitude and never diminishing energy and activity give credence to his statement. All of this suggests that growth is a never-ending process. While there obviously is some point in time when physical infirmity sets in, the fact is the normal person in reasonably good health can keep mentally active and continue to grow productively even at a very advanced age. *Each of us should accept the challenge to grow each year more than in any previous year of our lives.*

By achieving personal growth the leader sets the example for his/her followers. Looking at the converse, the leader who ceases to grow, who becomes "flat and dead," stultifies the vibrancy of the organization. As followers sense the personal growth of their leaders they derive a sense of excitement and a feeling of greater confidence in their leadership. Growth by the leaders adds tone and sparkle to the organization. It radiates a sense of movement and a confidence that the organization can cope with increasingly competitive demands. Remember, when you stop growing you begin to die.

The leader needs much more than integrity to be successful. But without integrity and trust nothing else matters much. In fact, integrity and trust are the foundation stones of all voluntary leadership.

A leader's values—the things he/she believes in and stands for—may be of greater significance than knowledge and experience. By values I mean integrity, trust, fair play, tolerance, pursuit of quality performance, and a desire for excellence—in brief, what you stand for, believe in, and live by.

It is imperative that we live our values and live them with consistency and courage. Nurturing and guarding our values better enables us in this changing and pressure-filled society to more clearly discern the constructive from the destructive, to distinguish what actions will provide a service and what may cause another or yourself to stumble.

Leadership not grounded in values and a deep sense of morality, leadership without ethics, leadership without a quality of concern for your followers becomes self-centered and self-serving; as a result, such leadership will lose its focus on building the organization and its people—the real purpose of leadership. Leadership not grounded in ethics will stifle the growth of new leaders and fail to generate a sense of trust and confidence in the followers. In brief, the ethical leadership of which I speak is based on the magnificently simple, but demanding Judeo-Christian principle, "Do unto others . . ." or the equivalent principles of any other faith. It is based on a deep and abiding concern for the welfare of the followers—it focuses on the primary task of helping people grow in stature and capacity so they can in turn contribute more and gain greater personal satisfaction in the process.

This, of course, raises the challenging question, "What role should ethics play in leadership?" Should there be some set of quality values and morality on which leadership is grounded? In other words, does the end purpose have any bearing on the effectiveness of the leadership? For example, is the leadership of a Hitler acceptable? Can one be a strong, effective executive in a business organization and still totally adhere to the Judeo-Christian principles (or those of some other religious faith)—or doesn't it matter? What are the moralistic, ethical, and societal responsibilities of a business executive or a leader of any organization?

Integrity is probably the primary attribute of an effective leader for, without it, little else will matter. To betray a trust is the unforgivable sin of the leader. A corporate president recently told me, "While it doesn't end there, any sound, lasting relationship must start with a basis of trust." Having a high degree of integrity requires that a person demonstrate over a period of time a consistent set of values, attitudes, and goals. As a result, the followers know by what criteria they will be judged and the kind of responses that will be forthcoming from their leader. This quality of personal integrity is the basis upon which mutual trust can be developed between the leader and the follower. And clearly, where the quality of mutual trust is absent, there is little basis for a following. In brief, trust born of integrity is an indispensable quality for inspiring people to follow. Joshua, who led the Israelites into the Promised Land in 1300 B.C., built his splendid leadership on the integrity of his word. It was said of him that he always kept his word. He was indeed a man of honor. The ultimate test of a leader is simply, "Can he/she be trusted?" It takes more, but without trust there is no foundation.

The leader builds trust essentially by first trusting; that is, he/she teaches his/her followers trust primarily by example. This quality is built on a foundation of openly communicating feelings, attitudes, and values. You do not profess honesty and trustworthiness—you live them. You must be what you represent yourself to be. These intangible attitudes are often as important as the actual business objectives espoused by the leader. Further, trust requires a quality of complete openness, and there can be no hint that the leader is playing games. He/she must listen to the points of view of others—and here listening means trying to understand. While he/she listens with understanding, the mature manager/leader does not vacillate where his/her principles are concerned. The leader must, however, honestly listen to other points of view and the followers must perceive that the leader has fairly considered them.

Finally, trust is being believable. It is the knowledge and the conviction on the part of the follower that the leader, though he/she may be tough, will never take advantage of his people or use them for selfish purposes. If one were to summarize in the simplest terms possible the core of President Richard Nixon's problems, it would be that trust in him by the American people ebbed away. The public increasingly realized that the president was not what he had pretended to be. There was a quality of relationship he formerly had which slipped away, and he found that trust and confidence had been the very heart of his capacity to do great things in his role as national leader—it was his wellspring of power. And later, regaining that trust or belief in the integrity of the office of the president was Mr. Gerald Ford's major platform. Interestingly enough, trust and believability were also the central planks in Jimmy Carter's program and every president's since.

Clearly executives of all ages are faced periodically by opportunities to make the fast dollar or gain increased power under questionable circumstances—actions that might deviate from the leader's consistent set of values. One question that should be carefully examined is what impact of short-term, quick gains may have on the long-term career of the executive leader. It is important to point out that life is more of a marathon than it is a sprint. Expressed another way, exerting quality leadership is not a quick thing. Rather, it is earned over time by consistent, high quality values in which the leader's whole life is an expression of service to followers and to the overall contribution of the organization as a whole.

One of the most demanding criteria for the high quality manager/leader is the unselfish, judicious use of power. It is axiomatic that the effective leader has power derived both from his badge of office and from his strength of character, personality, and intelligence. Managing power is a complex issue—a book in itself. Let me here touch on just two aspects of it.

First, the noble leader uses power unselfishly to enhance the organization and not himself. Power can hurt badly and deeply. Thus it must be used with a quality of gentleness and wisdom, though indeed it must be used because power is part of the leader's weaponry for getting results. Shakespeare, in his play *Measure for Measure,* gave us some wisdom on the use of power: "O, it is excellent to have a giant's strength; but it is tyrannous to use it like a giant." Indeed it is excellent and necessary for the leader to have power—in fact, by simple definition the leader is and has power. It is probably his/her most important and sacred trust. It is imperative that he/she turn it to lofty purposes—that his/her use of power should edify and exalt the organization and its people. If that sounds somewhat spiritual, it was meant to be. Using power is a lofty, heady business. It can destroy or build. Thus it must be handled sparingly with wisdom, good grace, and for unselfish purposes. As Napoleon said, "He who governs should possess severity without cruelty." The leader must be tough-minded and resolute not just for the sake of being tough, but only when it serves a high and useful purpose.

Second, the judicious use of power requires an intelligent distribution of power to others. Granting too little or too much power or granting it to the wrong members of the organization can undermine the effectiveness of quality leadership. The important point is that the leader must share his/her power in a thoughtful, unselfish way and grant power to those who can handle it with maturity. In fact, a critical part of the developing leader is to learn (by help from his/her leader) how to use power and responsibility with wisdom and grace.

Indeed the wise exercise of power is the mark of a high quality manager/leader. Thus leadership is not for the timid or the selfish, for neither can handle power with edifying effectiveness. Neither can take advantage of power in truly constructive and enlightened ways. *Leadership is for the unselfish and noble who can use power to enhance the effectiveness of the organization and the true growth of its people.*

A word of caution. I am not suggesting a "holier than thou" attitude or moralistic preaching. I am speaking about the leader making decisions and taking actions that are solidly and consistently grounded in a quality set of ethics. And I have little use for some scholars who demur, arguing who is to decide what the ethics are—who determines the ethics? Taking that position is a cop-out. Every culture, every society has a religion or a set of traditions that sets forth a set of ethics and a creed by which to live—to work and play. Our culture in this country was founded and shaped by the Judeo-Christian principles. These should form the basis for quality leadership. While we often fall short, the leader must ever keep these ethics before him as a model for shaping both the substance and style of his/her leadership.

There has been much in the press about important CEOs having their ego getting the better of them. One executive recruiter suggests that there are many CEOs whose egos have caused them to lose control of their companies. One psychologist suggests that a CEO needs a sizable ego to cope with the job. Clearly some leaders with large egos develop a sense of divinity—a belief in their own invincibility. Increasingly they do not listen and often lose touch with the key people in the organization. I believe one way to keep the ego in reasonable check is to never lose sight of the need to be the servant leader. The leader who is sincerely concerned about growing and developing his/her people, about being dedicated to feeding the troops will keep his/her ego under healthy control. It is vital for the ego-driven leader to always keep before him/her that *the leader's role is not to be served but to serve.* The leader should ever keep before him that simple statement on the Prince of Wales' crest, *Ich Dien*—"I serve." That is the only way I know to keep a healthy ego under good control.

It is always difficult to say that one period in our history is less moral than another. Let me rather look at the present and project it into the future. Unethical practices are evident in every sector of our society. Every one of our important institutions has had its showcases of questionable ethics—in some cases deplorable ethics.

- The corporate world has had unusual displays of greed ranging from embezzlement to excessive executive compensation and "golden parachutes" that in some cases are flagrantly undeserved. And the rash of takeovers and leveraged buyouts have demonstrated excessive greed by a few who want it now and let someone else pay for it later.
- In government, in the military, in politics—the press is full of accounts of shabby performances by our leaders.
- Universities and hospitals have had some shameful experiences of the mishandling of funds and authority.
- Perhaps most shocking of all have been the low-level antics of some of our most sanctimonious church leaders.

Are these isolated cases that represent such a small percentage of society that we need not worry? Are they more or less than seems to be the norm for human organizations? I have no definitive answer to these questions. My intuition says that these cases of unethical practice are too frequent and too pervasive to be ignored. Yet we know by definition that the Homo sapien is less than angelic. Humankind has and will err, cheat, and lie. My theme is simple. The most important distinguishing characteristic of the leader is that his/her ethics, the values by which he/she lives, set him/her apart. *Unquestioned nobleness of ethics is the critical mark of the good leader.*

Obviously quality leadership has many requirements. At the least it demands a keen understanding of the surrounding geography and what is necessary to travel through to the achievement of goals. However, the spirit and the drive of the organization, ingredients so crucial to success, are nurtured and enhanced by adhering ceaselessly to demanding ethics. If our leadership in 2000 and beyond is found inadequate it is most apt to be more because of failures in our ethics and morality than it will from inadequate business smarts. Our shortcomings will be (and have been) more those of character rather than of intelligence.

The fact that leaders will continually falter and fall short must not alter the quality of our vision. It is imperative that our leaders at all levels strive to be the ethical servant leader. In this way such servant leaders will be consumed by the desire to increase the ability of their followers to perform, to grow, and to contribute. While some (or all) may falter, having the vision of the servant leader before them is crucial to our organizations—yes, to our society.

The bottom line is clear. Managing and leading our institutions has become increasingly difficult and complex. The need for bringing about change is growing. All of our institutions, business, government, hospitals, universities, and churches face an uncertain future. There will be continued change and turmoil with less predictability. Managerial leadership will need newfound maturity and flexibility to act and react. There will be a need for unusual imagination and new kinds of skills will be required.

We are facing an environment that will be less forgiving of mistakes. Manager/leaders can clearly win or lose depending on their own capacity to cope with the new, tough demands. There will be an increasing premium on good, quality managerial leadership. Certainly our new manager/leaders will need greater knowledge and understanding of the technical aspects of information processing and decision making. In today's competitive world markets, leaders must understand the complexities of the marketplace. There are increasing pressures and uncertainties and resulting changes required in the leadership of our institutions—government, church, hospital, and educational. Managing and leading in the computer, information technology era will take keen intellects and a lot of smarts. Never before has the quality of leadership been so critical to organizational success. This is what led me to say early in the book that perhaps the *last frontier open to us will be our ability as leaders to increase human effectiveness. The ultimate ingredient for successful leadership will not be technical understanding but rather our capacity to use technology to help us get important things done through our organization.* As important as that is in our knowledge driven society, the real payoff in managerial leadership will be the capacity to increase human effectiveness by unleashing the power of the organization—getting more that is beneficial done through leaders and subleaders throughout our institutions.

This leads into my basic theme in this book—the *ultimate purpose and test of leadership is to unleash the power of your people.* The crux of this challenge is to build the team—*to achieve more human effectiveness through team building.* I remember some years ago saying that our society needs more corporate heroes. Heroes will probably always be a wish—somehow we have a wishful thinking about the business heroes of the late nineteenth and early twentieth century. In our nostalgia we long for their return. Certainly the media and the historians find them more interesting to write about than the servant leader in the high-performing organization.

But what we need, in our global society, are quality leaders—thousands, perhaps millions—at every level in our society, throughout all our organizations. The squad leader over ten becomes critical in the marketplace or in the factories. And to paraphrase Jethro's advice to Moses, we must have leaders over tens, fifties, hundreds, and thousands. Not necessarily heroes but multitudes of leaders who can transform each unit and thus the whole organization into an effective, highly competitive team. It will be the ability of our leaders to forge such effective teams that will decide how the United States and the free market world performs in the worldwide economic competition as we move into the twenty-first century.

There is no quick or easy way to summarize my beliefs about managerial leadership. The risk is always that important concepts by definition will be excluded. Clearly leadership is too complex and even mysterious to be capsulized in a few words. Despite these risks I will recap this treatise on leadership by highlighting my primary principles on the subject.

○ Character is the vital ingredient to voluntary leadership and followership. And at the core of important qualities of character is integrity. Trust indeed is the cornerstone—the foundation—the sine qua non for effective leadership.
○ The highest stewardship and most sacred trust of leadership is the judicious use and distribution of power and responsibility.

The noble leader will not be perceived to take personal advantage of power but will rather direct it to the enhancement of the organization and the growth of his people. When Shakespeare said, "O, it is excellent to have a giant's strength, but it is tyrannous to use it like a giant," he gave wise counsel to leaders. But beyond these moralistic concerns is the need to possess the wisdom and maturity to know how much power and responsibility to give to whom and under what circumstances. Understanding this is much more art than science.

○ A third tenet of good leadership is to live and serve and govern based on a consistent set of quality values. The leader must live his/her beliefs and values and must be consistent in their application. These qualities must be unselfish, uplifting, and edifying to the organization—a source of motivation and enduring inspiration.

○ The exceptional leader must understand and live the concept of the servant leader. By this I mean he/she must serve his/her people—nurture them in their growth—and as I discussed earlier in the book, "feed your troops, and serve first that you may command better." The servant leader nurtures the capacity of his/her people to produce at a higher level, while growing in the process and gaining deep satisfaction by being able to contribute more to the organization.

○ I agree with the generally accepted concept that managers and leaders are not exactly the same. Where I differ with many current scholars is in my strong belief that these qualities can be combined in the same individual. Hence it is more meaningful to use the term manager/leader because to be truly effective there must be a combination of both the skills and attitudes of the manager and of the leader and the inherent sense of the right balance to bring to bear on any organizational task.

I must say again that any person with reasonable intelligence and basic qualities of character (which many people have—more than we think) can develop into an effective manager/leader. What this suggests is that leaders are more developed than they are born.

As a final message, let me suggest a series of important criteria for judging the quality of a manager/leader. This of course can be used for self-appraisal as well as judging others. This is another way of looking at what constitutes an effective manager/leader. Many would agree that the major determinant is the success achieved by the leader's organization; that is, what successes has the leader led the organization to accomplish? However, to add perspective and an additional dimension to your thinking it can be helpful to reflect on the leader's performance capabilities in terms of the following eight criteria. Under each criterion several questions are listed to test the "stuff" of which the manager/leader is made.

1. Decision-making will and capacity.
   - To what extent does the manager/leader feel comfortable in making difficult decisions both about people or finances and decisions with either or both short- and long-term risk?
   - What have been the leader's most significant decisions? What was his/her process for making them—analytic or "gut feel," or some combination of these? How well does he/she handle and balance each approach? What have been the results of such decisions?
   - Is his/her process rational and understood by the organization? Does the staff understand how to contribute to the decision-making process?
   - What is his/her awareness of the impact of such decisions on people and situations? Does he/she appreciate what might result and can he/she handle the consequences?
   - Can the leader handle with good grace the stress of tough decision making?

2. Expectation level and demands placed on followers.
   - How high are the demands the leader places on himself/herself? And how hard does he/she push himself/ herself? To what extent does he/she want to excel?
   - What are his/her demands on others? To what extent are they met?
   - How intelligently does he/she apply pressure to himself/herself and others?
   - How hard and effectively does he/she hold people to targets? That is, what is his/her degree of toughness?
   - When the leader makes high demands, to what extent does he/she follow up to help the people increase their capacity to produce?
3. Quality of the image which the leader creates.
   - What is the image the leader projects to his/her subordinates, to peers, and to those above?
   - What kind of response does he/she stimulate from people throughout the organization?
   - To what extent is he/she viewed as a natural leader?
   - If the leader did not have the badge of office, how would he/she be viewed? Under those circumstances, to what extent would he/she be followed?
4. Personal drive and ambition.
   - What achievement level in the organization is necessary to satisfy him/her, that is, how high does he/she have to go?
   - What is the leader's level of stamina and endurance?
   - How does he/she handle adversity? Can he/she keep coming back to do battle?
   - What is the leader's capacity to sustain effectiveness over long periods of stress?
5. Intellectual fiber—the desire to grow.
   - What is his/her capacity to continue self-education?

- In what specific ways has the leader grown?
- What is his/her curiosity level, his/her zest to learn new things?
- What is his/her capacity and desire to explore new technologies or alternative management processes?
- How hard can he/she argue his/her position and principles against tough opposition?
- Will the leader take a tough stand on difficult issues?

6. Capacity and potential to manage and lead.
   - What is the leader's capacity to conceptualize alternative corporate directions and translate them into practical programs?
   - What has been the leader's track record in developing managers under him or her? Whom has he/she helped and in what ways?
   - What has been the leader's success in developing management processes that increase the organization's capacity to be managed?
   - To what extent has the leader led through other leaders? Does he/she have people under him/her who contribute significantly to the decision making and forward progress of the business?

7. Attitude toward change.
   - What has the leader done to demonstrate his/her capacity and will to bring about constructive change?
   - What is the leader's level of confidence in handling change situations and how did his/her people respond to them?
   - Is the manager/leader a change seeker, a willing follower once the final decision has been made, or does he/she dig in and resist?
   - To what extent does he/she "turn people on"? Does he/she move and inspire followers?
   - Does he/she have a quality of integrity that is

above question?

- ○ Does he/she inspire others to performance by his/her own example and deeds?
- ○ Does he/she manage emotions with maturity?

8. Character above reproach.
    - ○ Does he/she exhibit unquestioned integrity?
    - ○ Is he/she a "big" person?
    - ○ Is he/she without arrogance?
    - ○ Is his/her ego well managed?
    - ○ Does his/her life edify and uplift his/her people?

As a final thought, Louis F. Gerstner, chairman of IBM, who is a fine student of management and certainly a top-notch business producer, believes "the difference between success and mediocrity in any organization can generally be traced to how well manager/leaders bring out the energies and talents of their people." In brief, the effective manager/leader knows how to unleash and guide the power of his people.

It obviously takes a great deal of smarts to truly produce in today's competitive world. But even more so it takes a lot of quiet guts, a goodly measure of wisdom, a strong set of ethics that will not loosely bend, and a lot of desire. It is hard to improve on Winston Churchill's admonishment—blood, sweat, and tears. But I might be bold enough to add three others—integrity, stamina, and the qualities of servant leadership.

These all make up the art and science of managerial leadership—and it is mostly art, and the end purpose is to unleash the power of people—to create the effective team, not just the corporate hero.

ABOUT THE AUTHOR

Robert P. Neuschel was a retired senior partner (in 1979, after thirty years) of McKinsey & Company, Inc., the international management consulting firm, where he served clients on all six continents in strategic planning, organizational management development, and logistics.

From 1979 on he was a professor of corporate governance at the J. L. Kellogg Graduate School of Management and served for twelve years as managing director of the Transportation Center, both at Northwestern University in Evanston, Illinois.

Neuschel served on a number of boards of directors of industrial corporations and nonprofit organizations. He served for ten years as a trustee of Loyola University of Chicago and on its medical center and hospital board. He served on the National Research Council's committee for the study of air passenger service and safety since deregulation. He served on the transportation technology agenda subcommittee of the National Defense Transportation Association. He also served on the coordinating subcommittee of the committee on petroleum storage and transportation of the National Petroleum Council, which advises the Secretary of Energy. He served for many years as a member of the executive council of the International Air Cargo Forum.

Neuschel served as a member of President Ronald Reagan's Transition Task Force in Transportation and was a special advisor to former Secretary of Transportation, Elizabeth Hanford Dole. He served as a member of the White House Conference for a Drug-Free America. He was a fellow of the Academy of Advancement of Corporate Governance. His biography appears in *Who's Who in America* and *Who's Who in the World*.

Robert Neuschel received a BA degree from Denison University, majoring in economics and English, and a master's degree in business administration from Harvard University Business School. He served in World War II for five years in the Army of the United States and was active in the New Guinea and Philippines campaigns in the Pacific Theater. He retired from active duty as a captain in the Army Air Corps.

Neuschel authored many articles on a wide range of management subjects with major emphasis on the processes of management, transportation logistics, leadership development, and the work of corporate boards. He also lectured extensively on these topics in the United States as well as in Europe, South America, South Africa, and Australia. He coauthored the book, *Emerging Corporate Governance,* which examines and evaluates recent changes in the role played by corporate boards of directors.

Robert Neuschel was a ruling elder of the United Presbyterian Church of America and active in its governance. He served as a trustee of the International Council on Education and Teaching.